The War in Iraq and Why the Media Failed Us

The War in Iraq and Why the Media Failed Us

David Dadge

Foreword by Danny Schechter

Westport, Connecticut
London

Library of Congress Cataloging-in-Publication Data

Dadge, David.
  The war in Iraq and why the media failed us / David Dadge ; foreword by
Danny Schechter.
    p. cm.
  Includes bibliographical references and index.
  ISBN 0–275–98766–3 (alk. paper)
  1. Iraq War, 2003—Mass media and the war. 2. Iraq War, 2003—Press coverage—
United States. I. Schechter, Danny. II. Title.
P96.I732U635   2006
070.4′4995670443′0973–dc22   2006015086

British Library Cataloguing in Publication Data is available.

Library of Congress Catalog Card Number: 2006015086
ISBN: 0–275–98766–3

First published in 2006

Praeger Publishers, 88 Post Road West, Westport, CT 06881
An imprint of Greenwood Publishing Group, Inc.
www.praeger.com

Printed in the United States of America

The paper used in this book complies with the
Permanent Paper Standard issued by the National
Information Standards Organization (Z39.48–1984).

10 9 8 7 6 5 4 3 2 1

For Al

CONTENTS

FOREWORD

This book tells an important story, an ongoing story, maybe even the story of our times. It's the story of a war aided and abetted by a nominally "free" media. It's the story of a war that was every bit a media war as a military undertaking.

David Dadge does us all a service by paying attention to the details of how the Bush Administration defanged critics in the media and managed the coverage of the run-up to the war and then the war itself.

It's all here—the bullying of reporters, the maneuvers to isolate and limit critical reporting, and the overall manipulation of the media environment. This book reconstructs how it was done, step-by-step, incident after incident, and crisis after crisis. The administration was skillful because it understood how the media business operates, how divided and competitive it is, and how news cycles work. Its media operatives understood "message disclipline" and how to engineer public perceptions and undermine any emerging counter-narrative that could effectively challenge the administration's storyline.

This was not just the work of the White House; it was dispersed through all the departments of government, including the Office of Global Communications and the specialists at the well-funded Intelligence and Information Warfare Directorate in the Pentagon.

They were all pushing a story line, shaped in part by an understanding that Americans like stories more than facts. That's why Hollywood narrative technique has been so successful, especially in an era of the decline of journalism as a serious force in American life. Moviemakers fictionalize reality with a well-plotted story structure, character conflicts, and happy endings. What the Bush people set out to do was to displace a fact-based system of information with a faith-based one. They did it by demonizing enemies, domestic and foreign, and then setting themselves up as a paragon of patriotically correct trust. The horror of 9/11 was skillfully used to achieve this goal.

How did the watchdog become a lap dog? Most of the press didn't bark in part because it no longer sees that as its role. This administration worked hard—and with the connivance and complicity of many in the media, it must be noted—to transform the historic concept of the "Fourth Estate" into what war commander Tommy Franks called a "fourth front" in his war plan.

Classical democratic theory posits a system of checks and balances, where the branches of government work like clockwork to confront each other when needed and insure that the public interest is protected. We all learned about that in school: the Executive proposes, the Congress disposes, and the Supreme Court assures that the Constitution is in command.

The Founders of the Republic understood that these checks would not always balance or restrain the power of the other. So they conveyed a constitutional right to a free press in hopes that a vigilant media would add an extra layer of protection.

One by one, these institutions that pretended at democracy began to fail us.

Imperial presidencies emerged with larger-than-life leaders arrogating to themselves powers and postures that were profoundly un-democratic. Throughout our history, many fell on their own swords or through self-inflicted scandals. They lied, made war, and overstepped their roles. And today even the processes of our elections seem flawed and untrustworthy.

The Congress was not far behind, whether controlled by Dixiecrats, Democrats or Republicans. Special-interest lobbies ran policy from the shadows in the cloak-rooms. Compromises and deals often doomed democratic hopes. Seniority turned some members into dictators and power grubbers. Today, the lobbyists on K Street seem to have more power than most elected representatives.

The Supreme Court has shown its capacity for partisanship and decisions that enshrine the power of the wealthy and conservative classes. Just think about the *Bush* v. *Gore* decision of 2000, which set the stage for what was to follow and made a highly questionable "selection" on flawed grounds by invoking an amendment passed to protect the slaves of an earlier era.

And of course, often in the background and the foreground is the real power center of America that was not foreseen in its current form when the Constitution was handed down by a group of white men of property: the powerful corporations behind the military-industrial complex that President Eisenhower warned us against fifty years ago and the military-industrial-MEDIA complex that David Dadge warns of today. Corporate power is often the least scrutinized and understood.

In a globalized economy, state actors and governments are no longer the key decision makers. Private interests are. Is it any wonder that public life is becoming privatized too? Or government propaganda? How else can we understand the role played by Fox News Channel and all the right-wing talk shows that function as an echo chamber for GOP claims? In the absence of a countervailing media outlet, they push all of the media to the right. Many tried to "outfox" Fox. Others self-censored themselves for fear of being attacked as apologists for terrorism.

And what of the press in this mix? Edward R. Murrow's famous saying, "Good night, and good luck," should be taken literally, as a metaphor for our media's role, not just as a farewell.

As media was corporatized and its ownership concentrated, journalism, the stuff of watchdogging (to turn a noun into a verb) became more a memory than a reality.

In their book *Our Unfree Press*, Robert W. McChesney and Ben Scott take a march down that memory lane with a collection of media criticism dating back to 1906 showing that the decay of the journalistic imperative to be the kind of watchdog David Dadge and so many of us yearn for has a long and inglorious history. The days of the Watergate investigation are long gone, and in 2005, one of its brightest stars, Bob Woodward, himself became embroiled in a media scandal. (He too was among the editors of the *Washington Post* who admitted that his paper had not done all it could have to challenge the Bush administration's march to war.)

So where does this leave us?

Study the chapters in this book and weep, but also understand the practices he describes so skillfully didn't stop with the war and haven't to this day.

If war is politics by other means, then politics is also war. That's what we are seeing today in the extreme partisanship that plays out on all the talk shows where heat is preferred to light and confrontation displaces conversation.

The war coverage had a template guiding it. Make a claim. Reinforce it with experts, usually the same ones over and over again. Marginalize all dissent. Narrow the range of debate. Use emotive language inciting fears. Make the only option "us" versus "them."

What was once considered Pavlovian and then Orwellian is today Bushian. The same media techniques that exaggerated the threat posed by Saddam Hussein later exaggerated the threat of a Kerry presidency. The same sales techniques that sold the invasion of Iraq with repeated catchy phrases, well-designed backdrop, and hype dominated the discourse.

David Dadge's study lays out the problem, with perhaps more of an emphasis on the role of government than my own work on the subject. But all media critics are left with an issue that journalists and scholars of all stripes are uncomfortable with.

What can and must be done by citizens to challenge these practices? Hoping that "the media" will rediscover their historic mission may be naïve.

In my view, we need to make media an issue, not just a complaint. We need to use books like this in campaigns to challenge media outlets and government propagandists alike. This means exposing these practices and challenging their practitioners.

As I write, the war on Iraq continues, and its coverage leaves a lot to be desired. As the editor of a media watch website Mediachannel.org, I am calling for a campaign to tell the truth about the war.

Here's part of our call to action:

As public opinion shifts, the media will shift too. It is already starting to, although not quickly enough. Many media outlets remain out of step with the public because they are in lockstep with the war.

Readers and viewers are rebelling against what they've been seeing and reading. Viewing levels on TV news shows are down and newspaper circulation is down as well. There is a reason that some "fake-news" programs outdraw "real-news" programs.

One by one, the newspapers and journalists that backed the war are backing down. The pro-war media consensus has cracked, and not just because Judith Miller of the *New York Times* now admits she was wrong, wrong, wrong. Miller was not alone in pumping the rationale for war, and even as her muddled story comes out, there are bigger fish to fry in the higher ranks of media corporations where "group-think" rules.

There is now an opening to press the press and move the media to change the political climate by challenging politicians to abandon a war that has already been lost.

The media has the power to do it and we have the power to move them to do it.

There are many proposals for more intensive monitoring and direct action, from protests to letter (and e-mail) campaigns.

If this book angers you—as it should—then you have a responsibility to join this fight.

David Dadge has told us what's wrong. It's our job as citizens to make it right.

Danny Schechter

ACKNOWLEDGMENTS

Although the process of writing a book is often a lonely one, the publication of a book is the collaborative effort of a great many people.

With this in mind, I would especially like to thank Hilary Claggett, the Senior Editor, who first saw the wisdom of *The War in Iraq and Why the Media Failed Us* and who persuaded Praeger Publishers to publish it.

My thanks also go to Erin Ryan and Bridget M. Austiguy-Preschel at Praeger Publishers who also assisted with the book's production, as well as the project management team at Newgen.

My Indexer Laura Shelley also deserves praise for her contribution. Laura not only produced an excellent Index at short notice, but also assisted in a number of other ways to improve the finished book.

As ever, special thanks goes to the Director of the International Press Institute (IPI), Johann P. Fritz, for allowing me to write this book.

It is also worth noting that the views expressed in this book are purely my own and do not necessarily reflect the views and opinions of IPI.

INTRODUCTION

"Is there any point to which you would draw my attention?"
"To the curious incident of the dog in the night-time."
"The dog did nothing in the night-time."
"That was the curious incident," remarked Sherlock Holmes.
                         —"Silver Blaze" by Sir Arthur Conan Doyle[1]

THE WATCHDOG THAT FAILED TO BARK

In the short story "Silver Blaze" by Sir Arthur Conan Doyle, the fictional detective Sherlock Holmes solved the mystery of a stolen racehorse after appreciating the importance of a dog's failure to bark! For Holmes, the inaction of the dog was the first link in a chain that led to a solution of the case; as he comments to Watson, "I had grasped the significance of the silence of the dog, for one true inference invariably suggests others."[2] In many ways, the American media's behavior, both prior to, and during the war in Iraq is not dissimilar to that of the dog in "Silver Blaze."

Given a watchdog role within American society—a role supported by the First Amendment and a raft of Supreme Court cases—the American media failed to ask the tough questions of an Administration that seemed determined to go to war. Instead of questioning the assertions about Weapons of Mass Destruction (WMD), especially Iraq's alleged nuclear weapons program, and Saddam Hussein's links with al Qaeda and the September 11 attacks, the media, as a whole, appeared silent on these issues. They often failed to remind their audiences that statements made by senior officials of the Bush administration were hotly contested, or a matter of conjecture. Even those media organizations that did question these views, often reported them in such a way that they gave credence to the Bush administration's views, while downplaying the views of those who disagreed. The consequence of this failure was a confusion in the American public's understanding of the Iraq war.

The distortions in the public's understanding may be seen in a number of polls taken by various organizations starting in 2002. Conducted before President Bush's October 7, 2002 speech in which he laid out the justifications for war, the poll by the Pew Research Center and the Council on Foreign Relations showed that 66 percent of people said they believed, "Saddam Hussein helped the terrorists in the September 11 attacks." Moreover, 65 percent of those interviewed said they believed Iraq was close to having a nuclear weapon, while 14 percent said they believed Iraq already possessed these weapons.[3] Another poll taken, nearly one year later, in September 2003 by *Time*/CNN reinforces the impression of Iraq's complicity in the September 11 attacks. The poll showed that almost seven out of 10 people believed in Iraq's involvement.[4]

This confusion continued after the war in Iraq was over. A poll carried out by the University of Maryland in March 2004 found that 57 percent of Americans believed that Iraq provided substantial support to al Qaeda before the war. Perhaps even more worryingly, 60 percent of Americans believed that pre-war Iraq had WMD. The belief in Iraq's weapons capacity existed despite statements to the contrary made by David Kay, who led the allied hunt for such weapons in Iraq, and Hans Blix who headed the United Nations Monitoring, Verification and Inspection Commission (UNMOVIC) before the war.[5]

Nearly two years after the start of the war, a Harris Poll in February 2005 found that 36 percent of Americans continued to believe that Iraq had WMD before the war started, and 44 percent still believed Iraqi nationals were involved in the hijacking of planes on September 11, 2001.[6] The public's stubborn belief in Iraq's participation in the September 11 attacks remains firm despite the explicit rejection of this claim by the 9/11 commission, which covered every possible aspect of the attacks.

If the polls point to misconceptions, they also highlight the media's failure to provide the truth to the public. While the Bush administration gained considerably from the belief that Iraq had WMD and was involved in the September 11 attacks, it is the media that helped communicate this impression to the public. After all, it is mostly through the medium of television, Internet, and newspapers that the policies of government are delivered. So the question arises: how did the faulty messages about Iraq get through without the Bush administration's assertions being tested? Where was the balance and context in the media's reporting that should have helped shape the debate in late 2002 and early 2003? Why did the watchdog fail to bark as the United States prepared to go to war?

Chapter 1

THE ROAD TO AWE

We've been waiting 49 days for the inspectors to find something. Today they finally found something, but is it really anything?

—Greta Van Susteren, *On the Record*,
Fox News, January 17, 2003

"I HAVE HERE IN MY HAND"

At an evening engagement on February 9, 1950, Senator Joseph McCarthy gave a speech that was to transform his political career. Speaking at the Lincoln Day dinner of the Ohio County Women's Republican Club, held at the Mclure Hotel, Wheeling, West Virginia, McCarthy was quoted as saying:

> While I cannot take the time to name all of the men in the State Department who have been named as members of the Communist party and members of a spy ring, I have here in my hand a list of 205 that were known to the Secretary of State as being members of the Communist party and who nevertheless are still working and shaping the policy of the State Department.[1]

With its explicit declaration that communists were working at the heart of government and the claim that the Secretary of State was actually aware of this, McCarthy's Wheeling speech was the catalyst for a sea change in American political life. By concentrating on the fear of Communist infiltrators in the minds of the public and government officials alike, the charges placed the Truman administration on the defensive regarding the threat, led to a series of events that were to have a wide-ranging and corrosive effect on American society for decades to come, and identified McCarthy as the leading anti-communist giving him considerable political power for four destructive years.

Although it has been argued that McCarthy's comments immediately set the nation on fire, the reverse is true. Despite their inflammatory nature, his sweeping claims took some time to seep into the public consciousness. According to Edwin R. Bayley, in his excellent *Joe McCarthy and the Press,* only 18 newspapers used the Associated Press's (AP) story on February 10.[2] Of these newspapers, 12 were from Wisconsin, while the best-known newspaper to use the story was the *Chicago Tribune.* A further 10 newspapers used a United Press (UP) story on February 11. Bayley also reported that the newspaper headlines were largely factual: "Charge 205 Reds in State Dept." (*Racine-Journal Times*) and "State Department Has 205 Commies, Senator Says" (*Nashville Tennessean*).[3] It was only later that McCarthy's words would become headline news across the United States.

Almost from the start, McCarthy began to subtly change his story. Giving a press conference at an airport in Denver, Colorado, on the day after the Wheeling speech, the Senator informed the assembled reporters that he held a list of 207 "bad risks," which he was happy to show them; however, the names were in a suit left on a plane. During the news conference, McCarthy failed to make an explicit connection between the individual cases and Communism.[4]

Later, in Salt Lake City, when giving a radio interview to a reporter, McCarthy used a figure that was wildly different to those used in Wheeling and Colorado. In answer to the reporters' questions about Communists he said, "I stated I had the names of 57 card-carrying members of the Communist party."[5] He then said he would provide the Secretary of State, Dean Acheson, with the names. The radio interview was carried by AP and, according to Bayley, encouraged a further 25 newspapers to report the story. Headlines included, "McCarthy Charges in State Dept. Hold Red Party Cards" (*Washington Star*) and "57 Commies in State Dept., Says Senator" (*Boston Herald*).[6]

On McCarthy's return to Washington, on February 20, he read into the Congressional record a copy of his Wheeling speech, which differed from that recorded by a reporter who was present in the town. The most important difference was the number, which now said, "I have in my hand 57 cases" and the charge which now read, "loyal to the communist party." Moreover, the text of the speech no longer said that the Communists were "known to the Secretary of State." McCarthy was changing the facts to suit himself and it came at a time when there was growing national media interest in his claims.

Between the Wheeling speech and his return to Washington, McCarthy toured the country giving a Lincoln Day Dinner speech to guests and reporters. On these occasions, he used a speech similar to that inserted into the Congressional record. Tireless in his own cause, the speech generated newspaper headlines wherever McCarthy went. In California, after a press conference at the Greater Los Angeles Press Club, the *Los Angeles Times* ran the headline, "Senator to Name 57 Aides of Acheson Listed As Reds" while, after a speech in South Dakota, the *Plainsman* ran the headline, "Odds Against U.S. in Communist Fight."

Despite these newspaper headlines, which were either supportive or ambivalent, there were some newspapers deeply critical of McCarthy's unsubstantiated claims. In an editorial on February 14, the *Washington Post* used the headline, "Sewer Politics" and the *St. Louis Post-Dispatch,* under the title, "McCarthy Does Some Backtracking," said the Senator was changing his figures almost daily.[7]

However, it was McCarthy's six-hour speech in the United States Senate, on February 20 that gained him the greatest notoriety. As on previous occasions, the speech used different figures to support his claims. This time McCarthy referred to 81 cases of subversives employed by the government who had been refused security clearance or were connected to organizations associated with the Communist party. The Washington speech received media coverage all over the United States.

McCarthy's speeches and tireless traversing of the countryside, and his repeated changes of both figures and facts worked in his favor. He had managed to generate a national controversy that would dominate much of public life until his final humiliation before the Army hearings in late 1954.

How had McCarthy managed to overcome a tough and skeptical media? Significantly, the wire services, such as AP and UP, were at a particular disadvantage when dealing with his unfounded accusations. Responsible for providing stories to newspapers across the country, they were often fearful of upsetting newspapers that supported McCarthy. In consequence, the stories on McCarthy were often "Just the facts, Ma'am" reports providing information on what the Senator had said and where he had said it, but without background detail and lacking in attempts to analyze the truth of his assertions.

Time was also against the wire services. AP and UP had to work extremely fast to produce stories for their newspaper clients. The articles were often written quickly in order to make the following day's morning newspapers and, in the case of UP and the other services, they were often reliant on AP, which could offer better national coverage. This meant that for UP and some of the other services their own stories would often not reach the newspaper stands until the day after AP's. Reporters working for the wire services were, therefore, hard-pressed and often unable to follow up on other leads or introduce contrasting views in their stories. With their concentration on quantity as opposed to quality, the wire services played into the hands of McCarthy who saw newspaper headlines and the stories of his speeches as the main way to consolidate his power and communicate his views to the public.

Another difficulty, this time for the newspaper editors and reporters, was how to approach the story, particularly in that month between the Wheeling and Washington speeches. Of course this very much depended on whether or not editors were moved by McCarthy's words, but it also called upon them to make a judgment. Many failed in this respect with a number of newspapers choosing to report ambivalently or without any attempt to check the facts.[8] The failure, together with the raft of publicity grabbing news headlines that arose from this failure, only furthered McCarthy's ambition and persuaded him that at least some of the media could be bent to his will.

There was also a lack of hard-hitting editorials in that first month—a fact that seemed to be an extension of the ambivalence first shown by the media in writing news stories about McCarthy. The question of whether McCarthy was correct in his assertion that "card-carrying" Communists were infiltrating government called out for a series of editorials exploring the rationale behind this claim. However, with very few exceptions, this was not done, creating a missed opportunity to explain to readers what was happening. McCarthy's accusations called for swift rebuttals or more evidence, but, by and large, the editors of numerous local newspapers failed to do this.

McCarthy's tactics also hindered good reporting. As previously seen, McCarthy was willing to change the facts whenever the media were close to disproving them or undermining them. Hence, the rapid changes throughout the month of February 1950 in the number of alleged individuals involved, whether such individuals were Communists or merely "bad cases" or even "specific cases," and who was actually aware of these people working in government. First, the Secretary of State was aware of the Communist infiltrators, then he was not, then once again, he was. These changes in the facts made it extremely difficult for the media to keep pace with McCarthy.

With the facts scattered as if confetti, McCarthy would refuse to provide additional information. On occasion, he would give enough of the story to induce reporters to write about him, but would then hold back. Making matters worse, when reporters asked for a copy of his speech or for the names of those involved, McCarthy would hedge. Facing the media, the Senator would say the information was variously "in a suit on a plane" or only for the eyes of the Secretary of State or President Truman. All of this was done brazenly and it sent up a smoke screen preventing the media from pinning down the story.

Slightly unsure at first, and certainly unprepared for the initial publicity arising from his Wheeling speech, McCarthy was more surefooted as his campaign to "warn" the country went on. Parallel to this, he became increasingly more confident in his dealings with the media. In *Joe McCarthy and the Press*, Bayley describes an interview with a reporter in Reno, Nevada, where McCarthy named three or four well-known people as Communists. After the interview, the reporter, fearing a possible libel action, asked whether McCarthy would be naming the same individuals in his speech later that night because he wanted the Senator to go on the record. McCarthy replied, "Young man, I know more about libel than you do. I'm a lawyer."[9] If he could not persuade, he was capable of blustering.

Speeches made in faraway parts of the country also helped McCarthy and he did his best to take advantage. These speeches had a "blow-back" effect, first appearing in small hometown newspapers and then gradually appearing in city and national newspapers, while all the time gathering momentum and energy. McCarthy often gave speeches and interviews to local newspapers while on his way to larger venues in the hope that the publicity of the event would follow him. With few exceptions this worked and it enabled him to gather support in those crucial first few months when he could have been exposed.

As Bayley notes, "The timidity of the wire services, the fear of controversy on the part of publishers, and an apparent lack of understanding of the importance of the issue by many editors worked to deprive many readers of full information."[10] Such concerns also prevented reporters from piercing the veil of deceit that McCarthy had wrapped around himself. As a consequence, the media failed to expose McCarthy in that first month between Wheeling and Washington, when he was at his weakest. The toll on American life for that failure was considerable.

However, while it is easy to blame the media, it should also be remembered that there were other journalists who worked tirelessly to chase down the facts and give their readers much needed background material; journalists such as Bayley, who worked at that time for the *Milwaukee*

Journal, Philip Potter at the *Baltimore Sun*, and Alfred Friendly and subsequently Murray Marder at the *Washington Post*. Sadly, there were very few journalists like these during a period when it was pivotal to contest every single claim made by McCarthy.

For much of the media, McCarthy represented a sheer cliff face that was almost impossible to gain purchase on. In that first month and shortly thereafter, direct attempts to pin McCarthy down during interviews led to prevarication and delaying tactics, making it difficult to chase down the facts about those accused and who knew what in the Truman, and subsequently the Eisenhower administration. After all, both sides denied what the other side said, leaving journalists to report from the sidelines. In the face of this, many journalists merely decided to report what was said, allowing claim and counterclaim to float back and forth. The "Just the facts Ma'am" approach held a seductive appeal for many journalists, and it was preferable to being overwhelmed by a sprawling story that reached into so many American institutions destroying the reputations of many Americans.

Perhaps the supreme problem for the media was the following: How does the media report on issues where it is difficult or impossible to verify the truth of what is being asserted? For those newspapers and journalists arrayed against McCarthy, it was not merely necessary to dispute the claims, it was necessary to catch him in an outright lie. But, in a story involving so much deceit, subterfuge, as well as questions of national security, this was not always possible. Even with the combined might of several of the country's best newspapers, later joined by the television networks, it was not until the Army hearings that McCarthy was brought low. That was four years later. The fact that McCarthy's reign lasted so long is a tribute not only to his media skills, but also to the difficulty of disputing his claims.

The impact of McCarthy led to significant changes in the media's methods of reporting. There was a general move away from purely objective-based reporting and a greater attempt at informing readers. Journalists also sought a better balance between editorials and news. Twenty-years later, the media were riding high once again after their work on the Watergate affair and their reporting of the Vietnam War. Joseph McCarthy and his dubious accusations were forgotten, and the media had returned to what it knew best: investigating government and informing the public.

Only things have not returned to normal after the McCarthy period. Unfortunately, while some elements of style and approach have changed, the media's fundamental weakness about reporting the claims of politicians remains, especially when those stories are connected to war and questions of national security. Fifty years on from the stain of McCarthyism, the media faced similar dilemmas in reporting on the Second Iraq War and the comments of the Bush Administration: How do you assess politicians when you may not have access to information that allows you to make a sound judgment? How do you assess opposing claims without the information to verify either claim? How do you report on complex issues with limited newspaper space or television time?

To pose these questions is not to suggest that the Bush Administration practices a modern form of McCarthyism; put simply, it does not, but when the two events are compared many of the media's difficulties are the same. There are, however, two glaring differences: on the occasion of the Iraq war it was a government making the claims and, instead of a relatively unknown Senator from Wisconsin, it was the President of the United States who was leading the charge.

I'LL SHOW YOU FEAR IN A MUSHROOM CLOUD

On January 28, 2003, U.S. President George W. Bush gave the annual State of the Union address to an audience including the House Speaker, the Vice-President, and both Houses of Congress. In the speech President Bush set out the many reasons why America was prepared to go to war against Saddam Hussein and Iraq, and, turning to the question of home-land security, he raised the following spectacle:

> Before September the 11th, many in the world believed that Saddam Hussein could be contained. But chemical agents, lethal viruses and shadowy terrorist networks are not easily contained. Imagine those 19 hijackers with other weapons and other plans—this time armed by Saddam Hussein. It would take one vial, one canister, one crate slipped into this country to bring a day of horror like none we have ever known. We will do everything in our power to make sure that that day never comes.[11]

With its mention of chemical and biological weapons and links to the September 11 attacks, President Bush's words painted an apocalyptic vision of the future that was aimed directly at the American people and calculated to sway them over the war in Iraq. It attempted to bind together the September 11 attacks and Iraq using fear as the adhesive. The President of the United States was essentially saying that the threat of attack was the same and, if the situation were allowed to continue, the results would be the same.

Elsewhere, President Bush laid down other reasons for war; once again they were designed to impress upon the American people its necessity. Enlarging on his theme, President Bush said, "The gravest danger in the war on terror ... is outlaw regimes that seek and possess nuclear, chemical, and biological weapons." He then went on to justify his statement, "These regimes could use such weapons for blackmail, terror, and mass murder. They could also give or sell those weapons to terrorist allies, who would use them without the least hesitation."[12]

President Bush then went on to apply this thinking to the situation in Iraq and made a series of statements on biological, chemical, and nuclear weapons. On the subject of biological weapons President Bush said, "in 1999 ... Saddam Hussein had biological weapons sufficient to produce 25,000 liters of anthrax," that he had "materials sufficient to produce 38,000 liters of botulinum toxin." As for chemical weapons, President Bush said Saddam Hussein had "500 tons of sarin, mustard, and VX nerve agent," as well as "30,000 munitions capable of delivering chemical agents" and "several mobile biological weapons labs ... designed to produce germ warfare agents"[13] The message was clear: Saddam Hussein is a dictator who, in the words of President Bush, was "assembling the world's most dangerous weapons."[14]

Alluding to Iraq's nuclear capabilities, President Bush painted an even starker picture: "The International Atomic Energy Agency confirmed in the 1990s that Saddam Hussein had an advanced nuclear weapons development program, had a design for a nuclear weapon, and was working on five different methods of enriching uranium for a bomb." He then went on to say that according to the British government Saddam Hussein had recently sought uranium from Africa and that he attempted to purchase "high-strength aluminum tubes suitable for nuclear weapons destruction." A few paragraphs later, President Bush added the statement, "With nuclear arms or a full arsenal of chemical and biological weapons, Saddam Hussein could resume his ambitions of conquest in the Middle East."[15]

President Bush reinforced this array of terrifying imagery by arguing, "Saddam Hussein aids and protects terrorists, *including members of Al-Qaeda* (emphasis added)."[16] Based on the President's State of the Union speech, the wheel had come full circle with yet another explicit connection to the September 11 attacks. Because of that speech, in the minds of the American people, the war in Iraq was a core element of the War on Terror: Saddam Hussein was identified with al Qaeda and bin Laden as a threat to the safety and security of the United States.

The State of the Union speech was one of the pivotal moments in the Bush administration's attempt to influence public opinion on the Iraq War, perhaps only second to Colin Powell's February 5, 2003 speech before the United Nations. Prior to that, various members of the Bush administration and its supporters had made numerous speeches on the subject of Iraq. Of these, some of the most controversial involved comments about Iraq's nuclear weapons. The debate involved many senior cabinet members of the administration who used disturbing imagery to buttress their claims; claims that the International Atomic Energy Agency (IAEA) contested.

With their capacity to kill millions and destroy entire cities, accusations surrounding nuclear weapons and Saddam Hussein's attempts to obtain them were always going to receive maximum publicity. The Bush administration was quick to seize on their impact and use them to influence public opinion. Aside from the frantic diplomatic efforts and swings in public opinion that characterized the slow but steady march to war in January and February of 2003—when officials from the administration frantically sought to maintain public support both at home and abroad— the most important period leading up to the Iraq War was in September and early October 2002, before the Congressional vote on war.

During this period, senior officials from the Bush administration routinely took to the television studios. Speaking to Wolf Blitzer on CNN's *Late Edition* on September 8, National Security Advisor Condoleeza Rice said in answer to a question about the uncertainty of whether Iraq was pursuing nuclear weapons, "The problem here is that there will always be some uncertainty about how quickly he can acquire nuclear weapons, but we don't want the smoking gun to be a mushroom cloud."[17] On the same day, Defense Secretary Dick Cheney said on NBC's *Meet the Press*, "We don't have all the evidence, but enough of a picture that tells us that he [Hussein] is in fact actively and aggressively seeking to acquire nuclear weapons."[18]

President Bush also made mention of nuclear weapons in his remarks to the United Nations General Assembly in New York on September 12. The speech attempted to encourage other countries to rally round the American and British approach to Iraq. Speaking to the assembled diplomats, President Bush said:

Saddam Hussein has defied all these efforts and continues to develop WMD. *The first time we may be completely certain he has nuclear weapons is when, God forbids, he uses one* (emphasis added). We owe it to all our citizens to do everything in our power to prevent that day from coming.[19]

President Bush also used the "mushroom cloud" imagery when he gave a speech in Cincinnati on October 6, 2002. After detailing Saddam Hussein's nuclear weapon's activities, the President said, "Knowing these realities, America must not ignore the threat gathering against us. Facing clear evidence of peril, we cannot wait for the final proof—the smoking gun—that could come in the form of a mushroom cloud." Whether the threat was real or imagined the imagery was to have a powerful impact on the American population.

When sifting through these comments, it is clear the media provided a variety of different responses for their readers. Some newspapers were even dubious of the claims that Hussein was actively pursuing nuclear weapons. For instance, responding to the Bush administration's claims, the *Chicago Daily Herald* published the following headline in the news section, "Bush uses fears, not evidence, to justify Iraq war."[20] The article stated that there was no "evidentiary case" for war. *USA Today* was also unconvinced by Cheney and Rice and, on September 17, one of the paper's articles carried the headline, "U.S. assertions go beyond its intelligence; Questions raised on Iraq." The article said the arguments made by senior officials were contradicting other intelligence sources within the U.S. government.[21]

One of the biggest critics of the Bush administration's attempts to use startling imagery and overcooked intelligence was the Washington D.C. office of the *Knight Ridder/Tribune Business News* (KRTBN), which supplied stories to *Knight Ridder*'s newspaper empire, among many others. In the same way that reporters for the *Washington Post* and the *Baltimore Sun* checked every fact and pursued every lead concerning the claims of McCarthy, the Washington office of *Knight Ridder* sought to verify the claims of the Bush Administration. Attempting to provide balance to the story of Saddam Hussein's nuclear weapons, on September 13, the Washington office sent a story out with the following headline, "Bush's Speech Offers No Smoking Gun over Iraq." The article by Ron Hutcheson sought to place the claims of President Bush, Cheney, Rice, et al., against those of their critics and it provided a fair view of the opinions of the international community.[22]

While these represented fair journalistic attempts at examining the veracity of the Bush administration's statements on Iraq, a number of other newspapers provided headlines and stories that either followed *the official line* or had much the same impact on the American public. This was especially true of Cheney's comments about nuclear weapons.

On the day after Cheney's appearance, the U.S. newspapers contained stories with the following headlines: "Iraq Pursuing Nuclear Bomb, Cheney Argues" (*South Florida Sun-Sentinel*), "Cheney: Saddam after nukes; Top officials imply U.S. should strike before Iraq does" (*Chicago Sun-Times*), "Cheney: Iraq's nuclear work puts U.S. at risk" (*Duluth News-Tribune*), and the elongated, "Iraqi Nuke Looms, Says Bush Team; Top Administrators Stress Need to Remove Saddam" (*Orlando Sentinel*). In the United Kingdom, the *Daily Telegraph* used the following headline for its article, "Saddam is months away from a nuclear bomb," while the Reuters news wire carried, "US cites new evidence Saddam seeking nuclear bomb."

Coming after the end of the summer holiday season and prior to the Congressional vote, the comments and subsequent headlines were geared to have an impact on the public and Congress alike. Significantly, only a few days earlier, on September 7, White House Chief of Staff, Andrew Card, had been quoted in the *New York Times* as saying, "From a marketing point of view, you don't introduce new products in August."[23] Dripping with political cynicism, the statement announced that the Bush administration was now in the process of marshalling its arguments for war and reaching out to the public. The marketing of the war had begun and the media were to be the conduit for the discussion.

Again there were similarities to the problems faced by editors during the McCarthy era. As members of the Bush administration, and due to their responsibilities regarding national security and defense, Cheney and Rice had privileged access to intelligence assessments that were not readily available to the public. As a consequence, they could advance certain statements without necessarily having to justify them or, in the alternative, merely offer their own perspectives in the knowledge they would carry weight. The overriding question for editors was how they reported on these statements and tried to balance them.

Many of the newspapers often reported speeches and interviews uncritically. And, given the fact that many readers skim headlines or only read the first few paragraphs of a news story, the opening paragraphs of these stories had considerable impact on public thinking. In the *Tallahassee Democrat,* for instance, under the title, "Veep: Saddam wants nukes Administration making its case to the public" the opening paragraph read, "Saddam Hussein is aggressively seeking nuclear and biological weapons and the 'United States may well become the target' of an attack, Vice President Dick Cheney said Sunday as the Bush administration pressed its case for toppling the Iraqi leader."[24]

Adding to the impact of the headline and opening paragraph, the rest of the article proved to be equally supportive of the Bush administration. The third paragraph quoted Condoleezza's Rice's "mushroom cloud" imagery, while the fifth used a statement from Defense Secretary Donald H. Rumsfeld, "Imagine, a September 11 with WMD. It's not 3,000; it's tens of thousands of innocent men, women and children." Other paragraphs carried on in much the same fashion, reinforcing the overall impression. Later, Cheney was quoted once more for effect. "We know we have a part of the picture and that part of the picture tells us that he is in fact actively and aggressively seeking to acquire nuclear weapons."[25]

In an article of some twenty paragraphs, "critics" of the administration are finally mentioned, though not named, in the fourteenth paragraph. However, succeeding paragraphs rally round the administration by again quoting Cheney justifying potential war in the face of the critics. The Iraqi vice president is then quoted at the end of the article denying the claims made by the Bush administration.

Naturally, one newspaper article does not make a propaganda coup, but it does point to the influence it had on local news. In the case of the *Tallahassee Democrat*, the words of senior administration figures were given priority in a newspaper article that flattered the Bush administration's views without attempting to balance the story with quotes from various critics who had serious doubts that Iraq was pursuing nuclear weapons. Such articles were repeated in many newspapers across America.

National newspapers were also not immune from this approach. One of the most egregious examples of this type of administration-orientated journalism came from arguably the finest newspaper in the world—the *New York Times*. In an August 26 article titled, "Cheney Says Peril of a Nuclear Iraq Justifies Attack," Elisabeth Bumiller and James Dao gave Defense Secretary Dick Cheney a free pass when discussing his comments about Iraq's nuclear ambitions. The article amounted to little more than a showy advertisement for the Bush administration's commitment to waging war against Saddam Hussein.[26]

The opening paragraph of the article said, "Vice President Dick Cheney today presented the administration's most forceful and comprehensive rationale yet for attacking Iraq, warning that Saddam Hussein would 'fairly soon' have nuclear weapons." Having primed the reader, the second paragraph quoted Cheney saying, "[Saddam Hussein would] seek domination of the entire Middle East, take control of a great portion of the world's energy supplies, directly threaten America's friends throughout the region and subject the United States or any other nation to nuclear blackmail."

In a 31 paragraph article, the critics of the administration are not even mentioned until the fourteenth paragraph and only in the blandest of terms, "The speech appeared intended in particular to answer critics who say the administration lacks intelligence data on Iraq's nuclear abilities." Quotes from critics are reserved for the final paragraphs. Moreover, the mention of critics such as former National Security Advisor Brent Scowcroft is couched in terms of Cheney's own speech and his desire to engage with the naysayers. As a result, the critics are actually denied their own voice. Readers of the article would also have gleaned little knowledge about the actual debate regarding Iraq's nuclear weapons.

Although extremely difficult to quantify in real terms, it seems that these types of newspaper articles worked in unison with other forms of media to convince people that going to war was the right decision. In the case of the *Tallahassee Democrat* and the *New York Times* articles there was a threefold process at work. First, Cheney, Rice, Rumsfeld, or President Bush would make a speech that would be carried in its rawest form by radio, television, and newswires to people both in the locality and around the country. Second, such views would be amplified during television talk shows and in interviews, reaching the public in a second wave following on from the first. Third, after these media blitzes, articles mentioning the speeches and television interviews would slowly appear in local newspapers. Given these various communication methods, the "selling of the war"—with its explicit pictures of nuclear destruction and the deaths of tens of thousands—went extremely well for the Bush administration in August and September 2002.

Polls taken both before and during this period show an improvement in the public's willingness to accept the invasion of Iraq. A poll taken by the Pew Research Center for the People and the Press, September 12–16, found that 64 percent favored taking military action against Iraq.[27] This poll compares favorably with the CNN/*USA Today* poll taken in August showing 53 percent of people in favor of sending ground troops to the Persian Gulf in an attempt to remove Saddam Hussein from power. By the end of September, the same poll was showing that support for the invasion was at 57/58 percent. Despite the fact that support was fairly flat, the September 2002 "nuclear" comments from the administration kept support in the high fifties, preventing it from ebbing away.

The *Los Angeles Times* undertook a poll in late August that found 59 percent of respondents believed that the United States should take military action to remove Hussein from power.[28] The *Times* poll was followed by one taken by NBC News/*Wall Street Journal* that showed 77 percent of respondents considered Saddam Hussein a threat. Such polls were not misleading, the comments about nuclear weapons when added to those about chemical and biological weapons and Iraq's ties with al Qaeda, were turning the tide for the Bush administration.

After a poor summer in 2002, when critics of the war appeared to be making some inroads, those in favor of war were now ahead in the opinion polls. The finishing line of the domestic race—the Congressional vote for war—was not far away.

A report examining the statements of senior Bush Administration officials prepared at the request of Rep. Henry A. Waxman of California's 30th District and titled, *Iraq on the Record: The Bush Administration's Public Statement on Iraq* uncovered a worrying number of misstatements on the question of Iraq's nuclear weapons program.[29] The report, carried out by the Special Investigations Division, compiled a database of statements made by five senior officials on the subject of Iraq's nuclear weapons program, chemical and biological weapons, and ties to al Qaeda.

Rather than examining statements later proven to be false, *Iraq on the Record* concentrated solely on statements that could be shown at the time to be untrue. *Iraq on the Record* also did not "assess 'subjectively' whether the officials believed a statement to be true."[30] In total, *Iraq on the Record* found 237 misleading statements on Iraq's threat made by President Bush, Vice President Cheney, Secretary Rumsfeld, Secretary Powell, and National Security Advisor Rice.

In order to ensure objectivity, the report was peer reviewed by Joseph Cirincione, senior associate and director of the Non-Proliferation Project at the Carnegie Endowment for International Peace, and Greg Thielmann, former acting director of the Strategic, Proliferation, and Military Affairs Office in the State Department's Bureau of Intelligence and Research.[31]

Regarding nuclear weapons, *Iraq on the Record* found that President Bush made 14 statements "exaggerating Iraq's efforts to develop nuclear weapons, while Vice President Cheney, Rumsfeld, Powell and Rice made, 22, 18, 10 and 17 respectively. Significantly, Waxman's report includes a diagram showing the number of misstatements that reached a maximum peak in September/October 2002—exactly the time when the Bush administration was campaigning hardest to win supporters.[32]

An example of the type of misstatement quoted in the report arose from President Bush's speech in Cincinnati on October 7, 2002 when he said, "[t]he regime has the scientists and facilities to build nuclear weapons and is seeking the materials required to do so."[33] However, when giving a February 2004 speech, the then director of the Central Intelligence Agency, George Tenet said, "The National Intelligence Estimate said that [t]he activities we have detected do not, however, add up to a compelling case that Iraq is currently pursuing what INR [the State Department's Bureau of Intelligence and Research] would consider to be a comprehensive approach to acquire nuclear weapons."[34] Such a view was shared by the International Atomic Energy Agency (IAEA), which stated there was no indication that Iraq had a nuclear weapons program.

As is well known, the Iraqi Survey Group in Iraq was later unable to find evidence of the nuclear weapons program. If there was little or no evidence of Iraq's nuclear capacity and no consensus in the United States intelligence community about its existence why were the comments of the Bush administration not treated with greater skepticism in the media? Why did it appear that undue weight was given to these comments without sufficient attempts being made to investigate their veracity? While the statements seemed designed to encourage the media to investigate these matters for themselves, much of the media consistently failed to do so. The result was that the media floundered; unable or unwilling to see behind the statements or expose them for potential sales puff. Instead, as with McCarthy, much of the media retreated to its pre-prepared ground of merely giving space and airtime to Bush administration officials.

DRAWING WATER FROM THE POISONED WELL

Have the media come all that far since senator McCarthy gave his Wheeling speech? The events during the lead-up to the Iraq war would appear to indicate that little or nothing has changed: the media still find it extremely difficult to test the claims made about national security. Moreover, those problems are magnified when the claims are made by the President of the United States and his most senior administration officials.

Although it is difficult to say with absolute authority that the American public reached the conclusion that the war in Iraq was justified on the basis of news reports in the media, it can be said that the Bush administration's most coercive arguments—WMD including the threat of a nuclear bomb—were communicated directly to the public with little or no assessment of the worth of these statements.

To achieve this end, the Bush administration harnessed a media policy that relied on the media to report on a series of set pieces: State of the Union speeches, televised speeches to Congress, speeches to enthusiastic supporters, and appearances on key prime television shows. Such a policy called on the media to act as a conduit and did not rely on their ability to contextualize, question and expose contradiction. In the eyes of the administration, the media were merely a medium relaying a particular message.

Concerning set-piece speeches, the Bush administration made good use of the way in which the media reported on these events. Knowing that the broadcast media would report key sound bites in a vacuum, with little exposure to criticism, and that, therefore, the speeches were a means of reaching the public without facing critical opposition, the speeches were fashioned to achieve the maximum effect. Hence the allusions to mushroom clouds, nuclear bombs falling into the hands of terrorists and bacterial and biological weapons. After the speech, or elements of it, had been televised, the speech would appear in newspaper stories often with little or no context or criticism. Finally, senior administration officials would enter the television studios to reinforce the message.

In the television studios, the administration officials could make use of another weakness of the media. Given the fact that officials like Vice President Cheney and Defense Secretary Rumsfeld were making broad assertions based on national security, those interviewing them were often unable to break through the wall of mystique. Even attempts to use confidential sources against the administration's statements had little or no impact. In the face of the Bush administration's assertions, quotes from unattributed sources looked weak and ineffectual and could easily be brushed aside on the basis that they merely revealed a minority view. Another problem was the length of studio time for these discussions.

Taking advertising breaks into account, guests on television shows have little time to express their views and explain difficult propositions—concision is a byword in broadcasting and it requires strict discipline. The subject must also be one that can be reduced to a few well-chosen sound bites; long answers to difficult questions are often impossible in this medium. Therefore, while the Bush administration's views could be developed in this concise manner, for example, the threat of a mushroom cloud, the contra view often could not. It also takes considerable time to rebut arguments made in the name of national security, especially when facing an array of selective reports and quotes from intelligence sources.

As a result, those arguing against the Bush administration's position were always at a distinct disadvantage as they were forced to defend themselves against a premise that had already received considerable publicity and, to a degree, been accepted by the American public.

At the center of the Bush administration's approach, and it could also be seen in the way Senator McCarthy handled reporters, was the issue of control. While this traditionally lends itself to the way the administration controlled the media message, the 24-hour news cycle, it actually goes much deeper. With its national security apparatus, CIA, FBI, NSA, etc., the Bush administration was able to control the dissemination of the facts that underpinned its own arguments. Officials could make inflated claims about worst-case scenarios safe in the knowledge that access to the data was, for all intents and purposes, hermetically sealed. Obviously, there were individuals willing to talk off the record, but the absence of names undermined their credibility.

Once again the similarity with Senator McCarthy is enlightening. McCarthy took reporters' hunger for information and his knowledge of how the newswires worked to exploit the media and ensure that his message on anti-communism was widely disseminated. In the same way, the Bush administration used television broadcasts of speeches, interviews on Sunday news shows and articles in local newspapers, to build up momentum for their view that the war in Iraq was a necessity.

Courting the media's appetite for controversy, McCarthy made outrageous claims about the number of communists in the state department and elsewhere. He did so with no factual evidence to support his claims; instead, he chose to allude to lists revealing an ever-changing number of alleged communists: Lists that he refused to disclose in their entirety. In its desire to show the American people the necessity of the war in Iraq, the Bush administration used grossly inflated language of the dangers of Saddam Hussein and relied on fuzzy intelligence to justify these claims. In both cases, the media dutifully reported the stories without fully realizing the implications of doing so; after all, communists in the state department and the threat of mushroom clouds are understandably news!

In their reporting of the lead-up to the war in Iraq, the media found themselves trapped in a dilemma: If they chose to ignore some of the more heated claims of the Bush administration because they lacked factual support, they ran the risk of alienating their readers, listeners, and viewers because of the enormity of the story and the perceived threat to the United States; however, if they chose to report the story they were faced with the danger of communicating the Bush administration's message without having the necessary information to place the story within its proper context.

The dilemma was one that their predecessors in the 1950s had faced with Senator McCarthy who skillfully manipulated the media to ensure that his own claims were reported without proper balance. Facing this dilemma before the war in Iraq, many editors chose the path of least resistance and merely reported the claims of the administration. The problem for editors was that members of former administrations or unnamed sources could not compete, in the minds of the public, with a Vice-President.

Confronted with little in the way of factual information to balance stories, much of the media decided to treat the story the same way it would treat a story about a compelling social concern. This meant a cycle of pyramid stories in the newspapers with the most important facts at the top and any context placed lower down at the base of the pyramid. The trouble with this approach was that many readers took in the headline and the statements from the Bush administration without necessarily reading the story to the end. Moreover, while this approach might work for a social story on a tire factory or safety at work, counterbalancing statements at the end of a story on national security do not go far enough in placing such stories within their proper context.

Another feature of this problem is the tradition in American journalism of fairness—which may also be seen as the impetus towards balance. Journalists in American journalism schools are taught to provide balance to their stories not only for the importance of objectivity, but also out of a sense of fair play. It is a tradition that is not so prevalent in the journalism of other countries, for instance, British journalism, which often sacrifices the niceties of balance or fairness in the attempt to provide the reader with an often emotional or skewered in-depth analysis. Tough as American journalism is, this sense of fair play, of giving space to the other viewpoint, is a continuing theme and it is something that the Bush administration was able to use to its advantage.

The result of the application of the fairness principle is that all arguments receive a fair hearing. Rather than highlighting issues that are either strong or weak, this approach convinces the reader that two opposing views are of equal validity, despite the fact that one view may not be well supported. This is particularly true of many of the stories regarding Iraq's alleged nuclear weapons program. Articles on this subject often treated the Bush administration's assertions as if they were facts themselves, no matter how much they were disputed. In consequence, newspaper readers were left to read articles that, although balanced (and fair), failed to provide a nuanced view or an analysis as to whether Iraq was actually pursuing a nuclear weapons program.

Despite this, it also has to be acknowledged that the success of the Bush administration in reaching the American public with its message was also the result of the media's inability to gain critical inside information that ran counter to the administration's claims.

By their very nature, national security stories draw upon two important aspects of journalism: rigorous critical analysis founded on time consuming and often expensive investigative reporting.

The problem for the media was not whether it was capable of carrying out these fundamental elements of journalism—it is worth saying that these are both features of American journalism in other areas—but whether it could source the relationships and reveal the information necessary to do so on this particular subject. Unfortunately, when looking at the media as a whole, it was simply a bridge too far. While they could report what the Bush administration said they were not always able to unearth the information necessary to rebut the truth of its assertions or provide the necessary context.

The media also found themselves confronted by an elementary truth about national security and intelligence issues. While it is possible to say—through statistics and interviews—that the safety in a factory has improved or gotten worse, it is not possible to be so categorical about whether Saddam Hussein is pursuing a weapons program or has chemical or biological weapons. The problem, and it was one not only for the media, but also for the intelligence community in the United States, was how do you make such assessments when you have few contacts within the country and cannot enter the country to ascertain the truth for yourself?

In the absence of hard information, the media were always going to have to rely on the institutions of the U.S. government for much of their information. The problem with this reliance was that it drove the media back to the very institution that was claiming the need for the war in Iraq. As a result, the water being drawn from the well by the media was poisoned at its source. Some newspapers, particularly the *Washington Post*, the *New York Times*, and *USA Today* were aware of this, but considering their need for water, it did not stop them sipping from the tainted well!

Connected to the notion of the poisoned well is the Bush administration's own somewhat skeptical attitude towards the media. As mentioned, the Bush administration views the media as merely a conduit to the public and not as a check on government. This denial of the media's watchdog role has considerable implications for the American media.

Chapter 2

WHEN PRESIDENT BITES "WATCHDOG"

Were it left up to me to decide whether we should have a
government without newspapers or newspapers without
government, I should not hesitate a moment to prefer the latter.
—Thomas Jefferson, 1787

They [the press] don't represent the public any more than other
people do. In our democracy, the people who represent the
public stood for election.... I don't believe you have a
check and balance function.
—Andrew Card, 2004

LEAPFROGGING THE MAINSTREAM MEDIA

While unfair to him, it is probably true to say that the *Washington
Post*'s Dana Milbank is probably the Bush administration's least favorite
White House correspondent. Significantly, it has been reported that even
before the president had taken his oath of office, officials asked the
Washington Post to reassign him. Fortunately, the newspaper declined
to do so and Milbank, who earlier reported on the White House for the
New Republic, went on to write a series of hard-hitting articles that, on
occasion, enraged the White House.

Perhaps the article that caused the greatest anger among administration
officials was Milbank's October 22, 2002 report in the *Washington Post*
titled, "For Bush, Facts Are Malleable" examining the gap between
Presidential statements and the perceived truth on such matters as a
1998 report by the International Atomic Energy Agency (IAEA) on

Iraq's capacity to build nuclear weapons and the argument surrounding Homeland Security Legislation.[1] Milbank's article said that Bush's rhetoric had "taken some flights of fancy in recent weeks" and that "a president who won election victory underscoring Al Gore's knack for distortions and exaggerations has been guilty of a few himself."[2]

Stung by the accusations, someone described only as a "Senior Administration Official" contacted ABC's *The Note* and provided the following quote, "This was a story that was cooked and ready to go before any due diligence of the facts." The official then went on to refute many of the facts of the article and said Milbank was "more interested in style than substance"; he also claimed to have offered Milbank additional information, but had been turned down.[3]

Adding to the administration's criticism of Milbank's piece, then Presidential spokesperson Ari Fleischer commented that, while acknowledging that on one occasion the president's statements were imprecise, "The president's statements are well documented and supported by the facts.... We reject any allegation to the contrary."[4]

Milbank's reporting has also led to further reprisals and the journalist himself has said that the Bush administration has, on occasion, tried to "freeze" him out and refused to assist him in writing his articles. The journalist also faced difficulties with such matters as travel schedules. Another journalist is quoted as saying in the *American Prospect*, "They've been terrible to Dana ... from day one. On fairly innocuous things."[5] A previous article of Milbank's, about plans to exempt the Salvation Army from certain state and local anti-discrimination laws, led to the intentional release of one of Milbanks irreverent pool reports to a conservative publication.[6] The dissemination of the report was widely viewed as an attempt to embarrass the correspondent.

In Ken Auletta's book *Backstory: Inside the Business of News*, the *Washington Post*'s national political editor, Maralee Schwartz admits that senior Bush administration officials such as Ari Fleischer, Karen Hughes, and Karl Rove have all contacted her suggesting that Milbank is unsuited to his position. It is a claim that was flatly rejected by the newspaper's executive editor Leonard Downie, who supports Milbank's work.[7]

Aside from Milbank, the *Washington Post* has faced difficulties from the Bush administration regarding the reporting of other journalists. In 2003, Tom Ricks, the military reporter for the newspaper, faced criticism from Defense Department spokesperson Larry DiRita.

Reacting to a March 2, 2003 article stating that the higher echelons of the military were worried in the lead-up to the war in Iraq and that they had trained for the wrong type of war, DiRita sent a letter of complaint to the office of the *Washington Post*. When he received no satisfactory reply, DiRita took the unusual step of going in person to meet with Downie, and editors Steve Coll, Liz Spayd, and Mike Abramowitz. After the meeting, DiRita would only say, "I had a very good meeting with the editors at the *Post*, but I won't discuss the specifics. It was very constructive, very professional."[8] In their own comments following the meeting, the *Washington Post* expressed its full confidence in Ricks.

Jonathan Weisman, Economics editor at the *Washington Post*, is another journalist who has experience of the Bush administration's desire to control final copy. In March 2003, Weisman wrote an extraordinary e-mail to Poynter Online outlining his attempts to write a profile of the then chairman of the White House Council of Economic Advisors, R. Glenn Hubbard. To put Hubbard's tenure in perspective, Weisman sought comment from an economist in the administration, but was informed that the interview was to be deemed "off the record" and that if he wanted to use any of the quotes he would have to seek permission from the press office.

Following the interview, Weisman duly sought permission for a quote concerning President Bush's attempts to end the double taxation of dividends. The press office assented, but called for a minor change that led to some horse trading and finally ended with the agreement to a quote that had been amended not by the interviewee but by someone in the press office. Weisman later further paired down the quote leading to an accusation from the press office that he had "broken [his] word and violated journalistic ethics."[9]

In his e-mail to the Poynter Institute, Weisman wrote:

> I had, of course, violated journalistic ethics, by placing into quotation marks a phrase that was never uttered by the source. . . . I had also played ball with the White House using rules that neither I nor any other reporter should be assenting to. I think it is time for all of us to reconsider the way we cover the White House. If administration officials want to speak off the record, they are off the record. If they are on background as an administration official, I suppose that's the best we can expect. But the notion that reporters are routinely submitting quotations for approval, and allowing those quotes to be manipulated to get that approval, strikes me as a step beyond business as usual.[10]

Through the experiences of Milbank, Ricks, and Weisman, it is apparent that the Bush administration is not above attempting to sway the media. Moreover, it seems that they are also prepared to go beyond simply trying to spin a story. In Milbank's and Ricks' case, officials tried, through telephone calls, letters, and even face-to-face meetings, to apply pressure on media organizations to get them to either change their staff or to change their reporting stance. While such meetings may well be helpful, because they can lead to a clear expression of opinions by both sides, the cases of the Milbanks and Ricks leave the impression that there is something else at work, something more than a "constructive" conversation between two parties.

With the possible exception of President Kennedy, who had genuine friends among the media, other U.S. presidents have often expressed a disdain for journalists, but grudgingly accepted their role within American society. In recent times, the prevailing philosophy has been to the effect that on questions of policies and events, politicians and the media will usually go their separate ways. The decision to meet or to communicate directly with editors cuts through this largely traditional approach and carries with it the taint of an administration intent on oppressing individual media organizations. After all, the failure to include other organizations in the meetings has the inevitable effect of singling out the organization and giving the impression that it has committed serious mistakes.

Naturally, media outlets, especially internationally renowned ones such as the *Washington Post*, are no strangers to these pressures and have editors used to dealing with powerful, and often, overly sensitive administrations. Nevertheless, there are always two levels of communication in such meetings: The surface discussion—always regarded as polite and constructive by both sides—and the far deeper one that carries with it the overtones that the administration can, if it so chooses, make things exceedingly difficult for the media organization. Obviously, even though it was never elevated to anything other than pettiness, Milbank's treatment carried just such overtones.

For these reasons, face-to-face meetings between media and officials carry considerable risks for both sides. In the case of the media, it is the fear that the pressure may well encourage a different approach to reporting, or, at worst, possible self-censorship; while for the administration there is the real risk that it will look overbearing and censorious.

Wiesman's experiences, however, go further than somewhat clumsy attempts to influence media organizations, it is indicative of a desire, so far as it is possible, to have control over the finished product: a desire to ensure that the message contained in the article reflects that of the administration. This undue concern with image and message has led the Bush administration to be viewed as possibly the administration least friendly to the media and, at the same time, one of the media's most savvy manipulators.

A constant complaint among White House correspondents is the infrequency of the president's press conferences. In his book *Backstory: Inside the Business of the News*, Ken Auletta states that from the beginning of his first term up to January 1, 2004, President Bush gave just 11 solo press conferences.[11] The figure compares unfavorably with other presidents in their first terms. Martha Joynt Kumar, professor of political science at Towson University, Maryland, has provided the following figures for presidential solo press conferences: Dwight D. Eisenhower held 74, John F. Kennedy 65, Lyndon B. Johnson 80, Richard Nixon 23, and Bill Clinton 38.[12]

Placing the previous presidential figures for press conferences in perspective, an article on the *Democracy Now!* website also claimed that the president only gave two solo White House press conferences in the first 14 months of office: the first was one month after September 11, while the second was on the eve of the war in Iraq.[13]

According to Bush administration figures, the reason for President Bush's antipathy toward solo press conferences is the vanity of the media in front of the cameras. In President Bush's eyes the media questioning him are not engaged in the serious search for answers, but merely trying to trick him in order to obtain a story for their news organizations. Based on this perception, the media approach a press conference with predetermined views that he has described as "peacocking." Interestingly, when interviewed for Auletta's book: *Backstory*, Dan Bartlett, counselor to the president, appeared to give another far more revealing reason why the Bush administration appears to shy away from press conferences. In answer to Auletta's question about why the president gave so few press conferences, he said, "At press conferences, you can't control the message."[14]

Bartlett's comment is significant because it not only reveals the lengths to which the Bush administration will go to ensure that the message is properly communicated, without the interference of the mainstream media, but also the way in which a president, who obviously feels uncomfortable in formal surroundings, is protected by his staff. The desire to protect the president has led to a battle of wills, with both journalists and the president approaching the press conferences with their own scripts— known as talking points. The outcome has more to do with a choreographed dance than the parry and thrust of a press conference. In consequence, the solo press conferences given by Bush are always less than revealing.

Instead of facing the media in the glare of the national television lights, the Bush administration has chosen to meet the media on its own terms. One method that has caused considerable problems for journalists attempting to report on the Iraq war is the off-the-record background briefing.

While off-the-record briefings—where journalists may often use what is said but cannot reveal the name of the person saying it—have been a tool in the hands of successive administrations, they have been honed to perfection by the Bush administration. The briefings allow senior officials to go on record without revealing themselves and, it should be acknowledged, many journalists consider such briefings to be helpful because they provide quotes, albeit without the benefit of attribution. The Bush administration, however, has constantly used these meetings as a core part of its communications strategy and as a means of supplying the media with information that, if necessary, it can easily distance itself from.

In recent years, the briefings have led to considerable criticism from the media. Instead of talking openly to the media, many senior members of the Bush administration have chosen to remain hidden behind the anonymity of the background briefing.

Andy Alexander, the chair of the American Society of Newspaper Editors' Freedom of Information Committee and chief of the Washington bureau of Cox newspapers has said, "We have allowed ourselves...to get to a point where the national security advisor can have a background briefing with 50 reporters and not have herself revealed."[15] Ron Hutcheson, the president of the White House Correspondents' Association, has also spoken about his experience of turning up for an on-the-record briefing with the then National Security Advisor, Condoleezza Rice, only to find that someone else was giving the briefing and it was off-the-record. Hutcheson's response was to leave the briefing in protest. Sadly, no other journalists decided to join him.[16]

In addition to White House press conferences, the president has given very few interviews to the mainstream media. As of summer 2005, the *New York Times* has yet to interview President Bush, and earlier in the year *Los Angeles Times* reporter Edwin Chen said that his own paper had also been unable to obtain an interview. Chen was quoted as saying, "This White House doesn't need California, has no use for California politically...so we carry no clout."[17]

There have also been problems convincing Bush administration officials to go on the record. In an article written in 2005 by the managing editor of the *American Journalism Review*, Lori Robertson, Chen once again provides an account of the difficulties of working with the administration. Writing about stem cell research, Chen approached Dan Bartlett, counselor to the president, and Karen Hughes, a former counselor to the president and now undersecretary for public diplomacy and public affairs, for additional information on the subject. He was told that the two officials did not wish to discuss the subject until the president had spoken. Chen is quoted as saying that their reaction took his breath away.[18]

Talking about the Bush administration to the *New Yorker* magazine, ABC news anchor, the late Peter Jennings, recalled that while working on a story about a senior figure in the Bush administration, he was told that the story "had better be good." Although Jennings said he ignored the comment, he admitted it was a strong statement to make to a member of the media.[19]

Having given fewer solo press conferences than any modern president and managed to sidestep many of the national print media, in October 2003, the Bush administration gave an indication of where its true priorities lay. On October 13, President Bush provided exclusive interviews on the issue of Iraq with five regional broadcasting organizations. The decision was viewed by media commentators as an attempt to reach out to ordinary Americans without having to go through the mainstream media and, while it might appear welcome that President Bush recognized the importance of local media, it also revealed the administration's belief that the mainstream media can hinder attempts to deliver the White House's message.[20]

Overall, it is clear that the Bush administration is perhaps the most disciplined administration to ever sit in the White House. Its constant desire to remain on-message through the use of specific talking points, the rarity of unauthorized leaks from members of the administration, the use of off-the-record background briefings, and the lack of press conferences have made it extremely difficult for the media to carry out its normal function of holding the administration to account.

Moreover, this was particularly true during the lead-up to the war in Iraq. During this period, information was pivotal—it was needed for the public to have a greater understanding of the need for war; however, the media had numerous obstacles to obtaining this information and to a very large extent it failed in its attempts to give greater context about why the administration was seeking public approval for war.

The actions of the Bush administration raise the question why was it so intent on blocking media attempts to review the decision to go to war? Although it is tempting to say that the obstacles placed in the way of the media were strong evidence that the administration had something to hide—this may be true—but the reality is that its antipathy toward the media existed long before the war in Iraq had become a priority. Therefore, something else is at work! The answer is much more likely to be that, ignoring over two hundred years of accepted principle, the Bush administration refuses to accept the media's "check and balance" role within American society.

YOU DON'T SPEAK FOR THEM!

Traditionally, the media in the United Kingdom and the United States are often referred to as the fourth estate. The phrase is most often attributed to the English historian Thomas Carlyle who in his book *On Heroes, Hero-Worship and the Heroic in History* commented, "Burke said there were Three Estates in Parliament; but in the reporters gallery yonder, there sat a Fourth Estate more important far than they all."[21]

To many, the quote from Carlyle provides a definition for the media's historical relationship with government. It speaks of a higher function of checks and balances and implies that one of the media's roles within society is to investigate the policies and claims of government, and, where necessary, to hold elected officials to account for their actions. Furthermore, to a greater or lesser extent, successive presidential administrations have accepted this explanation of the media's role.

Naturally, these presidents did not always like the media nor were they necessarily comfortable with their role. Even a president as media friendly as John F. Kennedy, who could count on former editor-in-chief of the *Washington Post* Benjamin Bradlee as a good friend, was occasionally outraged by the reports appearing in the media. He once sought to have the *New York Times'* David Halberstam removed from Vietnam because of his reporting. By contrast, President Nixon had a more visceral reaction to the media and was not so mindful of freedom of the press that it prevented him from telephoning publishers to try and have journalists fired. President Carter also had a temperamental relationship with some journalists, while President Clinton developed a strong dislike of individual journalists for the way they reported on him.

Such problems are representative of the clash of strong personalities born of having to operate in a harsh and tough political world. Nevertheless, the fact that, in all these cases, the relationship between the president and the media endured is a sign that each accepted the role of the other. Operating with a very different mindset, the Bush administration has discarded this model and, as a result, has an entirely different relationship with the media.

Expressed quite simply, the Bush administration refuses to accept that the media is a vital check and balance on government and, more importantly, that the media acts on behalf of the American public. Instead, the Bush administration tends to view the media as another special interest group whose role is to supply sensational stories to further its own commercial concerns. Supporting evidence for this view may be found in comments made by the president and many of his most senior officials.

Originally appearing in the *New Yorker* magazine and later in his book *Backstory: Inside the Business of News*, Ken Auletta recounts the story of a journalist who, in answer to President Bush admitting that he rarely reads the news, asked him, "How do you then know what the public thinks?" The president replied, "You're making a powerful assumption—that you represent what the public thinks."[22] President Bush's belief is supported by his Chief of Staff, Andrew Card, who in answer to one of Auletta's questions said, "They [the media] don't represent the public anymore than other people do. In our democracy, the people who represent the public stood for election. . . . I don't believe you have a check-and-balance function."[23]

Tellingly, the shift in attitude toward the media has had a ripple effect. If you deny the media's Fourth Estate role and view them as a "special interest" group they can be marginalized, or even ignored. The shift is reminiscent of Dostoevsky's *The Brothers Karamazov* where a character in the book accepts the principle that god is dead and then assumes everything is possible! In the same way: accept the media have no role in holding government to account and there is no attendant duty to provide them with information. This shift is dramatic in its overall effect and deeply damaging to American society. It nullifies the media making everything possible. The new approach announces an era where government can introduce its policies and, if need be, block the scrutiny of its actions.

Perhaps more then any other area of the Bush administration's policy, this attitude had profound implications for the war in Iraq. Shorn of its watchdog duties, the media could be viewed as merely another obstacle to convincing the American people that the war was both correct and just. In consequence, the Bush administration could direct all its efforts to selling the war without having to justify it to the Fourth Estate.

To create this environment of acceptance, the Bush administration used keynote speeches to Republican supporters in the heart of the United

States, weekend rounds of television interviews, and the somewhat overblown language of mushroom clouds and the threat of biological and chemical weapons. In the face of this publicity onslaught, the media, with little access to government reports, and few chances to closely question the president or other senior members of the administration, found it extremely difficult to scrutinize the rush to war.

At this time, the media also faced a number of its own problems, especially in the lead-up and early months of the war when certain events conspired to undermine its ability to question an administration that may have overreached in its decision to go to war.

At the end of the Clinton administration the American public had become increasingly disenchanted with the media. Scandals, such as the Monica Lewinsky affair and Whitewater, were followed in exhaustive detail in some quarters of the press; such reporting inevitably led to a backlash against the media and a questioning of its credibility.

According to a study carried out by the Project for Excellence in Journalism in 2004, "Since 1985 believability of the daily newspaper has fallen by a quarter, from 80% in 1985 to 59% in 2002."[24] Alongside problems for the print media, the big three terrestrial broadcasters also suffered comparable dips in their own believability. Another study, this time carried out by the Society of Newspaper Editors in 1999, stated 53 percent of the public viewed the media as having few connections with the concerns of mainstream America.[25]

Maintaining the public's trust is another problem for the media. A 2002 Harris poll said that in comparison to journalists, the public had greater trust in clergy, teachers, doctors, police officers, the president, and even accountants.[26] The figures are disturbing for a profession that relies on its credibility in order to carry out its work.

In the early months of the war in Iraq a number of scandals involving journalists also served to undermine the public's confidence in journalism. The story of *New York Times'* journalist Jayson Blair, who not only plagiarized the work of other journalists, but also invented stories, damaged both the *Times* and reporting in general. Staff at the *Times* first became aware of Blair's unethical practices in April 2003 when the editor of the *San Antonio Express News*, Robert Rivard, sent e-mails to the then executive editor of the *Times*, Howell Raines, saying that Blair had copied material from the newspaper about a Texas woman whose son was killed during combat in Iraq. The revelations about Blair led to a series of events that culminated in the resignations of Raines and *Times'* managing editor, Gerald Boyd.

On May 1, Blair resigned and he subsequently wrote a letter of apology stating, "I have been struggling with recurring personal issues, which have caused me great pain. I am now seeking appropriate counseling...and I regret what I have done."[27] Later in May, the *Times* announced the formation of a staff committee to examine newsroom policies to ensure that the Blair episode was not repeated.

Furthermore, in order to allow staff to express their own views on the Blair issue a "town hall" meeting was held on May 14. Raines chaired the meeting and chairman Arthur Sulzberger, Jr. also appeared on stage. Unfortunately, Raines lost control of the rancorous meeting with staff bringing up a deluge of complaints about his management style. The meeting caused considerable embarrassment with other newspapers gleefully taking the opportunity to write about the *Times'* misfortunes. Having lost the confidence of his staff, it later transpired that Raines had also lost the confidence of Sulzberger and, on June 5, both Raines and Boyd resigned from the newspaper.

In addition to the resignations of Raines and Boyd, one of Raine's favorite journalists, Rick Bragg, was also forced to leave the *Times*. Bragg was originally suspended over questions of proper attribution, the notion of drive-by journalism, and a failure to give proper credit to assistants who worked on an article. One of the main accusations against Bragg was the questionable ethics of "toe-touching" whereby journalists fly or drive briefly to a certain location in order to be able to use the location as part of their byline. Although the practice is fraudulent in the sense that the journalist never actually reported from the location, the practice is not uncommon in journalism and there were many who felt that Bragg had been unfairly treated for doing what many others had done. Both the Blair and Bragg resignations led to a wide-ranging examination of journalistic practices at the *Times* and there were changes in reporting standards to try and ensure that the episode was not repeated.

Proof that the *New York Times* was not the only newspaper to suffer at the hands of unethical journalists, *USA Today* also found itself mired in a scandal that resulted in changes in its reporting practices. In May 2003, the newspaper received an anonymous e-mail about Pulitzer Prize finalist Jack Kelley questioning the journalist's reporting.

The e-mail led to a thorough investigation. At first, the inquiry focused on a July 14, 1999 article that claimed Kelley had seen a notebook containing details of ethnic cleansing in a village in Kosovar. Kelley claimed that his translator could corroborate his story; however, it later transpired that instead of corroborating his story the translator was merely reading from Kelley's version of the story. Believing that Kelley was deliberately obstructing the investigation, and doubtful that he could support his story, the journalist was dismissed. Subsequent investigations revealed other problems with Kelley's journalism and there was once again a series of resignations by senior management at *USA Today*.

Of course, such scandals, which were later followed by others as newspapers examined their own standards, are not uncommon. In 1981, the Janet Cooke affair, in which the reporter gave a fictionalized account of a young child addicted to drugs, scandalized the *Washington Post* and led to the reporter having to return her Pulitzer Prize.

Perhaps the most disturbing aspect of these scandals was that they arrived at exactly the time when the media were attempting to report on the war in Iraq. The scandals helped undermine the media, leading to introspection, which further hindered their ability to report. In the face of a strong and confident administration, the scandals made it exceptionally difficult for journalists to question the actions of the executive.

In essence, they could not have come to light at a worse time and their effect was two-fold. First, they reinforced the Bush administration's notions that rather than being a watchdog the scandal-ridden media was driven by poor ethical standards and a lack of concern for the truth; second, they reinforced the public's own jaundiced view about the media. It is common for journalists to say that it is their credibility that allows them to practice their profession. The various scandals shattered this perception for all journalists, often leaving them tainted by scandals that were unrelated to them.

With the credibility of the media being questioned by both the government and the public, the Bush administration was also in the process of tightening up another avenue that allowed for the review of government activities: the Freedom of Information laws.

THE MEDIA'S FIGHT FOR GREATER ACCESS TO INFORMATION

Almost immediately after September 11, the Bush administration started to restrict accesses to information held by the federal government. On October 12, 2001, the then Attorney General John Ashcroft issued a memorandum—later to be called the Ashcroft Memorandum—to all heads of government departments and agencies that reversed previous commitments to provide, where possible, information under the Freedom of Information Act (FOIA).

In his memorandum, Ashcroft reminded the department heads of the exemptions that existed under the law and invited them to consider whether "institutional, commercial, and personal privacy interests could be implicated by disclosure of the information."

If so, Ashcroft said,

> When you carefully consider FOIA requests and decide to withhold records, in whole or in part, you can be assured that the Department of Justice will defend decisions unless they lack a sound legal basis or present an unwarranted risk of adverse impact on the ability of other agencies to protect other important records.[28]

Ashcroft's decision brought to an end the more open policy of the Clinton administration which, under Attorney General Janet Reno, had called on the heads of departments and agencies not to use the exemptions unless the disclosure would lead to some "foreseeable harm." Commenting on the new approach to requests under the FOIA, *Access Reports* said the Ashcroft memorandum "reflects a movement back to the policy of the Reagan administration."[29]

Six days later, on October 18, with the Ashcroft memorandum firmly in mind, the Office of Information and Privacy reminded its own staff of the existence of a 1989 statement on freedom of information that stated exemptions connected "solely to the internal personnel rules and practices of an agency" could be applied to prevent anyone accessing vulnerable information. *Access Reports* said, "While there was as yet no evidence of willful manipulation of the FOI law, the memorandums set a tone by which the administration will be known."[30]

Following these moves against open access to information, President Bush signed into law Executive Order 13233 (EO13233) known as the "Further Implementation of the Presidential Records Act" in order to restrict access to historical presidential papers. The decision led to sustained criticism that the administration was seeking to prevent critics from evaluating its decisions. "There is a desire for fewer documents out of the door because they are withholding on principle . . . . This is not well founded in law," commented Jim Wilson, the chief counsel for the House Committee on Government Reform.[31]

Although subtle, the changes had a considerable impact on attempts to obtain information. According to the National Conference of State Legislatures, within six months of the September 11 attacks, there were almost 300 examples of federal, state, and local officials restricting access to information.[32]

With the emphasis on shielding information rather than allowing it to flow freely, there are a number of vital areas where journalists and members of Congress have been denied access. One such area involves the 9/11 commission's attempts to obtain information from the Bush administration concerning the September 11 attacks. On occasion, the commission has been frustrated in its attempts to gain information; however, as an indication of just how tight the Bush administration's grip is on certain types of information, members of the commission have complained that some information they have viewed should not have been restricted in the first place.

Interestingly, the chairman of the commission, Thomas Kean, has stated that much of the information he has reviewed often contained hearsay or was information that could be readily obtained elsewhere. As a result, the documents were not necessarily secret. Quoted in a news article Keane said, "Three quarters of what I read that was classified shouldn't have been." Lee Hamilton, the vice chairman of the panel previously known as the National Commission on Terrorist Attacks Upon the United States, said, "We've got a serious problem of over-classification."[33]

Another area where information is at a premium is under the Homeland Security Act (HSA) 2002. The law, which creates a new agency—the Department of Homeland Security (DHS)—tasked with coordinating all of the efforts to prevent a reoccurrence of the September 11 attacks, contains what are known as "critical infrastructure" provisions that protect certain types of information from being publicly disclosed. Under the protective provisions, private companies who provide information to the government regarding "vulnerabilities in the nation's critical infrastructure" are awarded a broad exemption from the FOIA. As such the law cuts through some federal sunshine laws and, according to Senator Patrick Leahy (R-Vermont), the provisions "shield from FOIA almost any voluntarily submitted document stamped by the facility owner as 'critical infrastructure.' "[34]

In 2004, two advocacy groups sought documents detailing how the "critical infrastructure" provisions were being used. When the DHS failed to respond, the groups went to a District court in Washington. Speaking about the litigation, Leahy said, "We learned that as of February 2005, the critical infrastructure program received 29 submissions and rejected seven of those. We know nothing of the substance of the accepted submissions, what vulnerabilities they may describe, or what is being done to address them."[35]

Elsewhere, the Department of Defense is also seeking a provision in a new law that would make it easier for the Pentagon to withhold information. Under the draft National Defense Authorization Act there is a provision seeking to ensure that "operational files" are immune from FOIA requests. Critics of the proposed provision have said that the Pentagon could potentially hide evidence of abuse or misconduct by claiming that the cases were still operational.

Once designated operational, the only way a file could become subject to the FOIA would be after a decennial or ten-year review of the file's public interest value; the proposal is similar in nature to the "operational file system" used by the Central Intelligence Agency (CIA). Using a somewhat disingenuous argument, the Department of Defense has tried to convince Congress of the need for the provision by arguing that the review of FOIA requests exhausts important man-hours that could be used elsewhere.[36]

In his October 12, 2001, memorandum, Ashcroft wrote, "It is only through a well-informed citizenry that the leaders of our nation remain accountable to the governed and the American people can be assured that neither fraud nor government waste is concealed."[37] The then Attorney General's words are well chosen, but it is clear that the Bush administration's information policy in recent years clearly negates the notion that citizens should be "well-informed" and that leaders are "accountable." The Bush administration's impulse has been to shield large amounts of information from the prying eyes of the public.

With its watchdog role of providing information to the public and holding government accountable, the media have been at the forefront of the attempts to wrench information from the Bush administration. However, as has been noted by Jameel Jaffer, an attorney for the American Civil Liberties Union (ACLU), in an atmosphere where civil liberties have been trumped by national security issues, "It's virtually impossible to get anything from the government without litigating, and even if you do litigate, you don't get everything that you want."[38] The media, like other groups has found the process of obtaining information extremely difficult.

The current situation has led to some ludicrous situations. For instance, in July 2004, *Forbes* magazine reported that a private party had been denied access to press releases on the issue of terrorism-related indictments by the justice department. Such attention to detail is proof that the changes in the approach to information have led to a growing bureaucracy where middle management is more intent on protecting itself rather than supplying information to the public. The consequence is a growing philosophy, as Jaffer points out, that departments should provide information only after the courts have forced them to do so.

Moreover, the debate over the public's "ignorance" or "awareness" is losing traction in an environment where both the war on terror and the war in Iraq have been brought together as one seamless problem. The composition of the current Congress is one that is very different from that which sat on September 10, 2001, and it is receptive to the arguments of departments that wish to maintain control over their information output. This in turn is fuelling a lack of awareness about critical issues among the public and allowing the Bush administration greater scope in formulating its policies without criticism.

BLOCKING ACCESS TO INFORMATION

In a departure from previous administrations, which accepted the watchdog role of the media, the Bush administration has deliberately set out to try and shatter this conception of a media operating on behalf of the public. Importantly, much of its information policy is founded on the belief that the media are not acting on behalf of the American people, but are, instead, merely another special interest group working out of commercial self-interest. The proof of this startling departure from the commonly accepted principle can be found not only in the Bush administration's refusal, with few exceptions, to grant the media access to its inner workings, but also in the comments on the media made by senior members of the administration.

The Bush administration has also tilted its own approach to the FOIA in such a way that the presumption is now that, where feasible, the heads of government departments can make every possible attempt to prevent information from being disclosed. This about-turn on the FOIA, considered to be one of the foundations of America's democracy, has allowed the Bush administration to control the flow of information and ensure, while keeping the media at bay, that it can successfully disseminate its own message.

Aside from information control, the media has also found it difficult to report on the war in Iraq due to the Bush administration's subtle manipulation of the environment in which the media works. Since the attacks on September 11, the administration has successfully managed to imply that dissent is anti-patriotic. This, in turn, has led to considerable pressure on the media to report the events of the war in Iraq in a way that is sympathetic to the Bush administration.

Chapter 3

DISSENT AND PATRIOTISM: THE ARM'S LENGTH PRINCIPLE

> But voice or no voice, the people can always be brought to the bidding of their leaders. That is easy. All you have to do is tell them they are being attacked and denounce the pacifists for lack of patriotism and exposing the country to danger. It works the same way in any country.
> —Hermann Goering, comments to Gustave Gilbert

THE SEPTEMBER 11 ATTACKS AND THEIR IMPACT ON DISSENT

Likened to Pearl Harbor during the Second World War, the September 11 attacks had a tremendous impact on the United States. The attacks sent seismic tremors through both the government and the public as it dawned on Americans everywhere that they were vulnerable to horrific acts of terrorism. In response to the September 11 attacks, the Bush administration slowly and cautiously set about forming international alliances, drawing up plans and eventually using military force to topple the ruling Taliban regime in Afghanistan and, in the process, destroying much of al Qaeda's infrastructure in the country.

At this time, the actions of the Bush administration won many plaudits from allies around the world and President Bush enjoyed extremely high approval ratings from the American public. However, with the public continuing to display anger at the attacks, the Bush administration often displayed a dislike for those who were prepared to criticize the administration.

One of the first signs of this attitude came with the administration's reaction to the comments of the host of ABC's *Politically Incorrect*, Bill Maher, who on September 17, 2001 said that the September 11 attacks themselves were not cowardly, but "lobbing cruise missiles" from 2,000 miles away was. Seen as an attack on the military, Maher's comments led to complaints from the public and the withdrawal of advertisers. Within months, ABC replaced the show.[1]

Commenting on what Maher had said, on September 26, 2001, President Bush's spokesperson, Ari Fleischer, said, "[I] t's a terrible thing to say ... [Maher's comments are] reminders to all Americans that they need to watch what they say, watch what they do. This is not the time for remarks like that; there never is."[2]

Fleischer's statement is extraordinary in that it implied that criticism of government was unacceptable during the period after September 11. He was essentially saying that there should be no dissent from the government during a time of crisis: while this view found support among the American public it also had a profound impact on the media.

Sensing that the American people were supporting their government's actions, the media found it difficult to continue with their role of holding the government to account. In the period after September 11, there appeared to be a need for a different approach: a form of journalism prepared to answer the questions of how the attacks were carried out, but which shied away from answering the question of why. Indeed, it was argued that the events of September 11 were so horrific and so traumatic that the public was unwilling to hear the answer to this question and certainly the public showed no interest in criticism of President Bush.

There is evidence for this in the way journalists, who criticized the Bush administration, were treated by their editors and publishers; actions that arose out of fear that the public backlash could damage the profitability of their media organizations. Writing for the *Daily Courier* in Oregon on September 15, 2001, Dan Guthrie said that, when viewed alongside passengers struggling with hijackers, "Bush hiding in a Nebraska hole becomes an embarrassment." After the column had been published Guthrie received numerous complaints as well as a death threat. Incensed by the column, publisher Dennis Mack fired Guthrie and insisted that the newspaper's editor apologize for the comments.

Guthrie was perhaps the first journalist to discover that the events of September 11 had changed the environment in which they worked, but there were other journalists who soon discovered that the same was also true for them. On September 22, 2001, Tom Gutting, writing in the *Texas*

City Sun, said President Bush, on the day of the attacks, had been "Flying around the country like a scared child seeking refuge in his mother's bed after having a nightmare." The comments led to a swift response from the newspaper's publisher, Les Daughtry, who promptly apologized for the comments and terminated Gutting's employment contract.

The treatment of these journalists was a sign to other journalists that dissent or criticism of the Bush administration was unacceptable. It marginalized critics in the media and narrowed the scope for debate about the September 11 attacks. When seen together the views of the public and Fleischer's comments made the position clear: journalists who criticized the Bush administration could lose their jobs.

Even those journalists who sought to encourage ethical journalism found themselves criticized, and not just from the public, members of the state legislature could also apply their own kind of leverage: financial pressure.

Following September 11, many television channels decided to use patriotic emblems to display their own support for the Bush administration's attempts to bring down the Taliban regime and find Osama bin Laden. Reacting to this, the station KOMU TV, a training station affiliated with the University of Missouri's School of Journalism, caused an outcry when it set down guidelines on the issue of journalists displaying patriotic emblems.

On September 17, 2001, Stacy Woelfel, the station's news director, sent a memorandum to the newsroom stating that it was the job of journalists to "deliver the news as free from outside influences as possible." The memorandum was leaked and Woelfel received e-mails from members of the state legislature informing him that, as a result of his memorandum, they would attempt to reduce the level of funding to the University of Missouri and the School of Journalism in particular. Such threats led to a wide-ranging discussion at the University, which eventually supported Woelfel's position. Woelfel kept his job, but the pressure on the career journalist was enormous and it once again revealed the depth of feeling existing in the United States.

Given this environment, many journalists felt the need to display their patriotic views. On September 17, 2001, the then CBS anchor and editor Dan Rather, when appearing on the *Late Show with David Letterman*, said, "George Bush is the president. He makes the decisions. As just one American, wherever he wants me to line up, just tell me where."

Although later in the interview, Rather said he had been too emotional, Rather's reaction was not uncommon among journalists who cast aside their impartiality to remain in lockstep with the American people. Adding his own voice to that of Rather's, Fox News owner Rupert Murdoch, who had become an American citizen, said that he was prepared to do his patriotic duty.

Another journalist rallying to the flag of patriotism was NBC anchor and Washington bureau chief Tim Russert, who was quoted as saying, "Yes, I'm a journalist, but first, I'm an American. Our country is at war with the terrorists, and as an American, I support the effort wholeheartedly."

The problem with these comments was that once the divide had been bridged, it was very difficult to return to being an impartial journalist. It was one thing to express patriotism, but those who did so ignored the danger that, with the Bush administration making use of the outpouring of patriotic sentiment, the journalists risked becoming identified with the policies and views of the Bush administration. The ultimate effect of this would be to undermine the journalist's credibility.

Facing an American public united by the events of September 11 and the continuing threat of terrorism, as well as a Bush administration determined to make use of the situation to pursue its own policies, the media found themselves operating inside a very small space. As a consequence, much of the media limited themselves to telling the news without answering the question as to why there were individuals determined to attack the United States.

As a result, dissent was essentially stifled in the United States with members of the Bush administration having contributed to the creation of what David Talbot, editor of Salon.com, described as a "censorious environment." The pressures on journalists to conform were acknowledged by the then chairman of CNN, Walter Isaacson, who said in November 2001, "In this environment it feels slightly different.... If you get on the wrong side of public opinion, you are going to get into trouble."

Having helped to create this environment the Bush administration then proceeded to reap the rewards. In the wake of the September 11 attacks, the government undertook a review of the country's security measures in order to combat terrorism leading to an adjustment in the delicate balance between security and civil liberties. One of the first signs of this change came with the passage of the U.S. Patriot Act, which was passed through the legislature within one month of the attacks and without the benefit of a committee report.

In the area of the free flow of information, the Bush administration slowly turned off various elements of this flow by attempting to restrict Congressional access to secret information, altering the government's policy on freedom of information laws, and ordering agencies to withdraw sensitive information from websites. In turn, state legislatures followed suit by passing laws limiting access to information.

Encouraged by public support the government also tried to introduce its Total Information Awareness (TIA) system free of Congressional oversight. An example of their confidence that the public would accept almost any change to the rights landscape, the Bush administration also floated the idea of the Office of Strategic Influence (OSI), a body apparently designed to spread disinformation among the media. While the plan was eventually abandoned, it was a sign of how just far the Bush administration was prepared to go in the War against Terrorism.

In turn, this created an information vacuum and it led to a considerable amount of misinformation—for example, the unfounded accusation that Saddam Hussein and Iraq were in some way connected to the September 11 attacks. Although during the intervening period between September 11 and the war in Iraq, there was some widening of this open space in which journalists worked, the open space was to close again before the war in March 2003 as patriotic expression rose and dissent was again pushed to the margins of American society.

How can the government manipulate the environment in which journalists work? To answer this question it is necessary to look back to the 1970s, as well as examine the media environment and, in particular, the relationship between government and the media.

LAW AND THE MEDIA

During the so-called golden age of a free press in the 1960s and early 1970s the battle for press freedom was largely with the federal government. Court cases such as *The New York Times Co. v. Sullivan* saw the U.S. Supreme Court setting the limits of defamation and defining the rights of "public figures," while in 1966 President Lyndon Johnson signed the ground-breaking Freedom of Information Act (FOIA), which was given additional teeth by Congress in 1974.[3] The high-water mark for the media came in the case of *The New York Times Co. v. U.S.* when the U.S. Supreme Court rejected the right of the Nixon administration to prevent the publication of the Pentagon Papers.

In his concurring opinion in *The New York Times Co. v. U.S.*, Justice Hugo L. Black said, "In the First Amendment the Founding Fathers gave the free press the protection it must have to fulfill its essential role in our democracy. The press was to serve the governed, not the governors....

Only a free and unrestrained press can effectively expose deception in government." Justice Black's words were not only a confirmation of the role played by the media in American society, but also an endorsement of its duty to watch over government. Significantly, since that time, the Supreme Court has not been called upon to hear another case of prior restraint involving the federal government.

With the courts dismissing attempts by the federal government to issue restraining orders on the media, the intervening years have seen the emergence of more subtle and vague forms of pressure. At the same time, the rise of companies—both national and multinational—have not only come to play a dominant role in American public life but also made it easier to influence the media and suppress dissent. Companies such as Coca-Cola, Microsoft, and Wal-Mart employ large numbers of people and exert tremendous power in communities throughout the United States. And, in the same way that corporate life has greatly impacted upon the life of ordinary Americans, it can also be said to have done much the same with the media.

Evidence for this may be seen in the huge rise in the amount of advertising expenditure from 1963, just prior to the Sullivan decision, to 1998. In 1963, an amount under $10 billion was spent on advertising, by 1998, the amount of expenditure had risen to $200 billion. With media companies largely in receipt of this expenditure, they have become increasingly dependent on it as a source of revenue. Furthermore, when this is seen in conjunction with a steadily falling federal work force and the growth in outsourcing and sub-contracting by the government, companies have increased in size and influence since the 1960s. A company such as Wal-Mart now has a gross domestic product of a country such as Chile.

Due to the entrenchment of companies in the surrounding communities, and their inter-relationships with the media, companies wield great influence on what does and does not appear in the media. However, the growth of companies has also had an additional impact. As a result of their growth, the increase in competition, and dependency on the public, they are at the mercy of changes in the public mood. Fearful of boycotts and bad publicity, companies have grown wary of antagonizing the public, particularly during times of conflict. This has led them, in turn, to be fearful of any dissent that shows them out of step with public expression.

And what of the government's approach to the media during this period, particularly in regard to conflicts involving the U.S. military? Once again, in the conflict zone, successive administrations have found it relatively easy to hinder the free flow of information. Dismayed by the media's negative reporting in Vietnam and willing to believe that it had played a role in the U.S. defeat at the hands of the North Vietnamese, the government aggressively controlled the media in the military campaigns that followed. Hence, in Grenada and Panama, the media were largely sidelined while, in the first Gulf War, restrictive reporting pools hampered journalists and prevented them from seeing the battlefront. Despite these successes, however, the government has not always found it easy to shape the home front in its own image.

With the Supreme Court refusing to assist the government, successive administrations have been left to apply other means to gain influence over the media and dissent. This has often involved the subtle application of pressure, calls for patriotism and a reliance on many commercial concerns to place profit ahead of the right of free expression.

While it may be said that the mix of these different elements amounts to censorship in the traditional sense of the word, it is a censorship by the government that has a distance and ambiguity to it that the question of prior restraint does not. The result is the emergence of a new form of censorship, equally malign, but undertaken at arms' length. Administrations are able to step back from the fray, disclaiming responsibility while stating that they are powerless to interfere. In this manner, the metaphorical hands of the government remain clean, while the much-desired pressure on dissenters is maintained.

The signature traces of this form of censorship may clearly be seen after the September 11 attacks which provided the foundation and the template for the Bush administration's methods in the lead-up to the Second Gulf War.

PRIOR RESTRAINT AND THE PENTAGON PAPERS CASE

Alongside the Watergate affair, the case of the Pentagon Papers is often perceived as a strong rebuttal of the government's right to seek prior restraint of what a newspaper publishes and one of the best examples of the media's willingness to fight an administration in order to pursue its right to hold high officials accountable.

Speaking about the Pentagon Papers in 2001, columnist Anthony Lewis said it was "the decision that, more than any other, established the modern independence of the American press—its willingness to challenge official truth. That was the decision of the *New York Times* to publish the Pentagon Papers."[4] In keeping with Lewis' views, other media commentators see the case not only as an affirmation of the media's role, but also as a case that had a transformative effect on the media revealing their true power in the face of a government determined to keep secrets. Based on this view, the Pentagon Papers case created a stronger, more independent media, that only a few years later, would have the confidence to expose President Nixon's misdeeds in the Watergate affair.

Looking back at 1971, when the Pentagon Papers were first published, there are broad similarities with 2003, the year of the Iraq war. Both were years in which America was at war and they were presided over by administrations feeling pressure over their involvement in conflict. But, the parallels end there. With the exception of a vocal minority, the war in Iraq received support from the American public and President Bush continued to maintain his high approval ratings long after the invasion. Moreover, in America, the Iraq war was largely seen as a pre-emptive strike borne of the necessity to prevent Saddam Hussein from acquiring WMD.

On the other hand, President Nixon found himself involved in a deeply unpopular war that was slowly exhausting the American desire to fight. By 1971, there was widespread public dissension and the Nixon administration was seeking an exit from the war, albeit one that would allow the United States to retain its credibility.

Written over a number of decades, the Pentagon Papers was a study of the United State's decision-making in Vietnam since 1945 and it contained a series of deeply embarrassing revelations concerning American foreign policy. Secretary of Defense Robert McNamara ordered the study prior to his leaving office ordered the study and those involved in its drafting were drawn mainly from the Defense department, other government departments and a number of contractors; the entire project was overseen by Leslie Gelb.

Completed in 1969 and classified top secret, the study was contained in 47 volumes and 7,000 pages. The pages included a detailed review of the history of the United State's involvement with Vietnam as well as 4,000 pages of attached documents in support. Only 15 copies of the finished study were made and the Defense department made every attempt to ensure that they kept a tight rein over its dissemination.[5] Due to its involvement in the project, however, two copies were provided to the Rand Corporation—a "think tank" that had worked on defense issues for over 50 years.

Although he had little involvement in the actual drafting of the Pentagon Papers, an employee at the Rand Corporation, Daniel Ellsberg, who had served in Vietnam as a high ranking civilian, was given access to one of the copies. Ellsberg's experiences in Vietnam had left him disillusioned with the U.S. participation in the war and, convinced that the government was keeping secrets from the American people, he sought to have the study published. When his attempts at convincing members of Congress to publish the study were rebuffed, Ellsberg made a secret copy of the Pentagon Papers and leaked much of it to the *New York Times* reporter Neil Sheehan.

Before receiving the documents, Sheehan had approached the chief news executive of the *Times*, A.M. Rosenthal, who said that, although he could not promise to publish documents he had not seen, he would not be swayed by the offence caused to the Nixon administration. Rosenthal also told Sheehan that his judgment of the Pentagon Papers would be made solely on their newsworthiness and their authenticity.[6] Reassured by Rosenthal's comments, Ellsberg provided a copy to Sheehan.

On receipt of the massive study, the *Times* created a task force to study the Pentagon Papers. After assuring themselves of their authenticity and agreeing to publish, the *Times'* lawyer, James Goodale, was told of their existence. Goodale's involvement set off a heated debate about what the government might be able to do to the newspaper and its other interests, including a television station. In the end, a compromise was reached between the lawyers on the one side, and the editors, on the other. It was agreed that they would publish only a limited number of the documents—about half the length of what had been previously envisaged.[7]

On June 13, 1971, the *Times* published an article on the Pentagon Papers. During the following day, Attorney General John Mitchell, via telephone and a fax machine, warned the *Times* against publishing any further installments. The *Times* continued with its publication and, on June 15, the Nixon administration went to a federal judge in New York and obtained a temporary restraining order subject to a full hearing.

What was to become a classic legal battle over the use of prior restraint between the government and the media had started.

Later in the month the *Times* would be joined in the courts by the *Washington Post*, who through its national editor Ben Bagdikian, was also able to obtain a copy of the Pentagon Papers. As had happened at the *Times*, the editorial staff at the *Post* entered into a heated debate over the First Amendment with their lawyers. Interestingly, one of the main fears for the *Washington Post* was the fact that on June 15, 1971, the newspaper had gone public and there were fears expressed that the legal fight with the Nixon administration could activate a clause in the share offering leading to a withdrawal of the sale.[8]

After the legal fears had been allayed, *Post* publisher Katherine Graham was called upon to make the final decision. Graham was placed in a considerable dilemma because, as the Nixon administration knew the *Post* had the Pentagon Papers, any refusal to publish could be used in court against the *New York Times*. In the end, after hearing both the editorial and legal arguments, Graham agreed to publish the study. In consequence, the Nixon administration found itself ranged against the two most prominent newspapers in the United States and the subsequent legal case would have a lasting impact on the relationship between the executive branch and the media.[9]

After hearings in the lower courts, the case made its way quickly to the U.S. Supreme Court. Initially, the Justice Department requested that argument be heard in a closed hearing, but this was denied and the case was heard on June 26, 1971. In its petition to the court, the Nixon administration argued that only the executive branch could make an assessment of the United States' security needs and that the restraining order should be granted on this basis. In their statements to the court, the newspapers argued that the imposition of the restraining order was a violation of the First Amendment and that the administration's actions were dictated by a desire for censorship and not a concern for national security.

Four days after the oral hearing, a six member-majority delivered a *per curium* (unnamed opinion) ruling that prior restraint carries with it a heavy constitutional burden and, in the case before it, the Nixon administration had failed to meet the burden. Commenting on the case, *Times* lawyer James Goodale said the decision of the Supreme Court "serves as a shield against an overzealous government."[10]

The decision was widely perceived as a success for the media and a defeat for the power of the government to prevent media organizations from publishing. However, the victory was not total because it appeared that the court accepted that an injunction could be issued if the government were able to meet the high standard of proving serious harm.

However, in the case before the court, it is likely that the majority of judges were not convinced that the release of the Pentagon Papers would cause any harm. On this basis, it seems the Nixon administration was actually involved in damage limitation; it did not want a study made public that revealed the mistakes made by successive administrations on the question of Vietnam.

This is supported by the Pentagon Papers themselves which show that the anti-colonialist United States had paid close to 80 percent of the failed French colonial war in the country; that the United States had undermined the 1954 Geneva accords; and that it had inflated the events in the Gulf of Tonkin in order to convince the public and Congress that increased involvement in the war was necessary. These acts, among many others, carried with them a considerable embarrassment factor, but they did not harm national security as suggested by the Nixon administration.

Another problem regarding the case is that each judge in the majority delivered his own opinion, making it extremely hard to discern the reasoning behind the decision. Given this difficulty, it is most likely that Justice Potter Stewart's opinion lays out the test that has to be met if the government is going to succeed with an action for prior restraint.

Justice Stewart in his opinion, said:

> We are asked, quite simply, to prevent the publication by two newspapers of material that the Executive Branch insists should not, in the national interest, be published. I am convinced that the Executive is correct with respect to some of the documents involved. But I cannot say that disclosure of any of them will surely result in direct, immediate, and irreparable harm to our Nation, or its people. That being so, there can under the First Amendment be but one judicial resolution of the issues before us.

On the question of the media, Stewart gave a powerful statement in support of investigative journalism. "In the absence of the governmental checks and balances present in other areas of our national life, the only effective restraint upon executive policy and power in the areas of national defense and international affairs may lie in an enlightened citizenry—in an informed and critical public opinion which alone can here protect the values of democratic government," wrote Stewart.[11]

Despite the Supreme Court accepting the principle of prior restraint, it does appear that the doctrine has little application against the media. This view has been upheld by the First U.S. Circuit Court of Appeals that described the heavy presumption against prior restraint as being "virtually insurmountable." As Goodale pointed out, although the courts have been willing to agree to temporary restraining orders, he said he was unaware of any cases where such an order has been "permanently granted."[12]

In terms of prior restraint for the purposes of national security, the government, therefore, faces an enormous uphill struggle and, given the value the Supreme Court places on the First Amendment, any action is unlikely to succeed. At present, the judgment in the Pentagon papers' case returns the legal position of prior restraint back to the earlier case of *Near v. Minnesota* (1931) that said, "Any system of prior restraints of expression comes to this Court bearing a heavy presumption against its constitutional validity."

Three years later, in 1974, during the Watergate affair, an ascendant media again challenged the executive branch of government and their work laid the foundation for the resignation of President Nixon. The investigations carried out by journalists in this period are viewed as one of the American media's finest hours and it helped to secure its reputation for decades to come.

The fact that the Nixon administration applied every possible pressure on the media, including, at one point, a direct threat against the other holdings of *Washington Post* publisher Katherine Graham, came to nothing. Investigations by the media could not be stopped and the confidence gained in the legal struggle over the Pentagon Papers enabled them to face down President Nixon over Watergate. With the Supreme Court having raised the bar so high regarding prior restraint, the executive branch in the Watergate case was deprived of a major weapon to prevent the publication of material that it described as having "national security" implications.

In consequence of these two cases, the fact that prior restraint against pure speech is merely a theoretical possibility raises an important question regarding the relationship between the media and the executive branch. For, if it is true that there is what amounts to a legal prohibition on governments directly preventing the publication of stories in the name of national security, how can governments influence the media to prevent these stories from coming to light? In effect, the legal decision, forces the government into an arm's length relationship with the media. How does it overcome this distant relationship to maintain influence?

The answer lies in the ability of a highly sophisticated administration to retake the media's "open space" gained in the hard-won battles of the 1970s by activating perhaps the most influential force operating on the home front during the time of war, namely the way in which patriotism can inhibit expressions of dissent and hinder investigations of the workings of government.

ROLLING BACK THE CRITICAL MEDIA'S INFLUENCE IN WARTIME

Any attempt to reduce the open space for dissent in a society during wartime incorporates the following three elements: Comments by senior administration figures that seek to show that dissent is unpatriotic; mobilization of the public's support for the comments made by the administration; and pressure on journalists from other elements of the media to support the administration's actions.

The application of these three specific factors, or, to be more precise, their triangulation, can force the media into a position where the pressure not to dissent from the administration's view is intense. In effect, these three factors have a coercive effect and, with very few exceptions, they undermine the willingness of journalists and media organizations to continue with the level of scrutiny applied during peacetime.

An additional pressure to be considered is the "exposure" factor of seeing what happens to other journalists who find themselves exposed to these types of forces. Too late, journalists such as Guthrie and Gutting discovered that the conditions for criticizing the Bush administration had undergone a sea change in the brief period between the September 11 attacks and the publication of their pieces.

In the case of Gutting, it is also worth mentioning that the publisher initially agreed to support his comments, but the guarantee of protection was withdrawn when he realized that the wave of public anger could be damaging to his newspaper. At that point, a clean break and apology were needed in order to rectify the damage and Gutting was thrown to the wolves. This is clear evidence that although a publisher's first instinct might be to uphold freedom of opinion, the pressures after the September 11 attacks were so great that they could not be ignored.

Of course, it is also possible to argue that as journalists, Gutting and Guthrie should have known that the time was not right for criticism of the president. But this view refuses to acknowledge the right of journalists to express themselves and, after the September 11 attacks, it seemed that the public was prepared to ditch the country's long cherished value of freedom of expression in order to show a united front.

Returning to those early months after the September 11 attacks, it is possible to see this process at work. Using Maher as an example, first, the Bush administration would criticize the act—as shown by Fleischer's September 16, 2001, comments—then there would be a backlash from the public as the story was reported, followed by commentary from supportive conservative media.

In Maher's case, there were calls from some parts of the conservative media for sponsors to withdraw from the show. Bowing to popular demand, this is exactly what happened with FedEx Corp. who quickly withdrew; later a number of affiliate television stations also refused to show *Politically Incorrect*. After much of the fuss had died down, ABC quietly took the show off the air and replaced it with a comedy show.

Regarding the Iraq war, it is obvious that similar forces were at work. If it is true that, according to President Bush, the war in Iraq is actually a part of the war on terrorism, it is also true that the events affecting the media after September 11 also influenced the media at the start of the war.

Returning to the question of the first factor, namely critical comments from the Bush administration aimed at separating dissenters from patriots, it is possible to see how the Bush administration worked to shape the environment in which the media operated.

Representing the Bush administration at its most belligerent and arrogant in its presumption that it could tell the American public to "watch what they say, watch what they do," Fleischer's comments were only the first in a series of comments that sought to marginalize criticism.

On December 6, 2001, the Attorney General, John Ashcroft, went almost as far as Fleischer. Speaking before the Senate Judiciary Committee about critics of the Bush administration's response to terrorism, Ashcroft said, "Your tactics only aid terrorists, for they erode our national unity and diminish our resolve. They give ammunition to America's enemies, and pause to America's friends."[13] These comments appeared to imply that critics of the administration were not too far away from being enemies of the United States, and his words chimed with the words of President Bush who a month previously had said, "You are either with us or against us in the fight against terror."[14]

Undoubtedly, these comments laid the foundations for the war in Iraq and they set the tone for an administration that refused to recognize that dissent was essential as a check on unrestrained government policy and action.

Both before and during the war in Iraq, the statements questioning the patriotism of critics continued. Many of the statements from administration officials or their supporters in Congress questioned the loyalty of dissenters or, like Ashcroft, said that the comments aided the enemies of the United States. Others implied that the comments endangered American soldiers fighting in Iraq.

On September 25, 2002, the then House Majority Leader, Tom DeLay, responding to criticism of the Homeland Security Department said, "These people that don't want to protect the American people. They will do anything, spend all the time and resources they can, to avoid confronting evil." DeLay's words were matched by Senate Majority leader Bill Frist, who in answer to appeals for a multilateralist foreign policy retorted, "Partisan insults launched solely for personal political gain are highly inappropriate at a time when American men and women are in harm's way."

One of the most direct attacks on the media's work came from the outspoken Secretary of Defense, Donald Rumsfeld, who, while on a visit to Iraq, said that the Bush administration's critics of the war in Iraq were encouraging terrorists and complicating the ongoing U.S. war on terrorism.[15] "We know for a fact . . . that terrorists studied Somalia and they studied instances where the United States was dealt a blow and tucked in and persuaded themselves they could, in fact, cause us to acquiesce in whatever it is they wanted us to do," Rumsfeld said.[16]

Continuing with the theme that the United States will not give up and that criticism aids terrorists, Rumsfeld said, "The United States is not going to do that. President Bush is not going to do that. Now to the extent terrorists are given reason to believe he might, or if he is not willing to, the opponents might prevail in some way . . . . And they take heart in that, and that leads to more recruiting . . . that leads to more encouragement, or that leads to more staying power. Obviously that makes it more difficult."[17]

The comments were made to journalists on a plane and, during the conversation, Rumsfeld made it clear that he was discussing not just the critical Al-Jazeera, but also elements of the western media.

Reminiscent of Ashcroft's comments before the Senate Judiciary Committee, Rumsfeld appeared to be implying that the media should have been giving President Bush their full support. His words called on the media to set aside notions that the American people deserved context or to hear both sides of the war in Iraq; instead their role was to act as the cheerleaders for the Bush administration and to ensure that support for the war did not drift.

The comment also contained the notion that, at heart, the Bush administration knew best. Such a view is also reflected in Ari Fleischer's reaction to criticism that President Bush's May 2003 aircraft carrier speech—mission accomplished—was inappropriate when fighting was still continuing. In response, Fleischer said, "It does a disservice to the men and women of the military to suggest that the president, or the manner in which the president visited the military would be anything other than the exact appropriate thing to do."

Rumsfeld's words revealed a misunderstanding of a modern reporter's job, but there may have been another reason for his comments. His words encouraged criticism aimed at those in the media who were undermining the war in Iraq and the war on terrorism, and they also mobilized the public. The comments could be seen as a signal for those supporting the administration to attack the dissenters. After all, according to Rumsfeld's view the criticism endangered the lives of soldiers.

Comments by administration officials had an impact on the American public and they helped energize support. In the lead-up to the Iraq war, there were two spikes in public support, the first during President Bush's State of the Union Speech in Jaunary 2003, followed by Secretary of State Colin Powell's speech to the United Nations. These speeches formed a pivotal role in communicating the Bush administration's case for war.

During his speech at the United Nations, Powell said, "The gravity of this moment is matched by the gravity of the threat that Iraq's WMD pose to the world. . . . This body [the United Nations] places itself in danger of irrelevance if it allows Iraq to continue to defy its will."[18] The comments had a considerable impact on the American people.

Polls at the time show that the American people supported the decision to go to war. A CBS poll, taken after Powell's speech, which was covered live by much of the world's media, showed that 70 percent of the American people were in favor of the military action against Iraq.[19] On the question of President Bush's personal ratings, prior to the war, his popularity stood at 53 percent, but on March 18, when war had been declared, his personal rating had increased to 68 percent.[20]

In addition to polls, the period before the war also saw a rise in patriotic emblems as the public began to throw its weight behind the government and the military. As had happened after the September 11 attacks, labels and pins appeared on people's clothes, while flags were unfurled. Once again, these expressions of patriotism further marginalized dissent and added to the pressure on critics. Sensing the public's mood, members of the conservative media, also aired their comments.

The opening up of a fissure between so-called conservative and liberal media is not a product of the war in Iraq, or even September 11, it has arisen because of increasing partisanship in American social and political life. With few examples of bipartisanship, the political scene has created an increasingly bitter relationship between Democrats and Republicans, fueled by the Reagan and Clinton administrations, which, in turn, led to the rise of partisan journalism.

Over recent decades, conservative media such as the Fox News Network in television, Clear Channel Communications Inc. in radio, and *The Washington Times* in print media have created a climate in the United States where expressions of dissent against a conservative administration have been met with stinging counterattacks. Adding to this pressure, there has been an increase in the popularity of conservative talk show hosts, both on radio and television. These commentators have made much use of their ability, cued by the statements of the Bush administration, to funnel public anger at dissenters. Further adding to the mix of voices on the conservative side, conservative bloggers, working outside the mainstream media, have also put journalists under pressure for their comments.

Moreover, the vituperative attacks are often not necessarily directed at the journalists themselves, but at the organizations they work for. This has been especially effective because in recent years a number of large conglomerates have purchased media companies. While in the past it could be said that criticism of journalism led to discussion about the improvement of work practices, in modern times the criticism is much more likely to encourage fears over the stock value of the parent company and worries about the loss of advertisers. In the modern media environment, commercial concerns have replaced professional concerns, and the Bush administration's supporters have exploited this change.

The result was a slow build-up of pressure and the creation of an environment where even some of the largest mainstream media have found it all but impossible to avoid reacting to the criticism. An example of how these pressures work could be seen shortly after the September 11 attacks, when the late ABC News Anchor Peter Jennings was castigated for apparently saying during a newscast that some presidents handle a crisis better than others. Jennings' alleged comments led to more than 10,000 e-mails, telephone calls, and faxes denouncing him.

On this occasion, ABC reacted quickly and released a transcript showing that the news anchor had been misquoted. Jennings was later vindicated. However, a similar situation did not end so well for CNN's Chief News Executive, Eason Jordan in 2005.

On January 27, 2005, Jordan sat on a panel at the World Economic Forum in Davos in Switzerland. During a discussion about the safety of journalism, Jordan said that he knew of 12 journalists who were killed by coalition forces in Iraq. Speaking afterwards, Rep. Barney Frank (D. Mass) was quoted as saying, "It sounded like he was saying it was unofficial military policy to take out journalists."[21] Responding to the criticism, Jordan later modified his remarks, but his attempt at explaining himself was not accepted and it led to a barrage of criticism from conservative bloggers and talk-show hosts.

Because the panel debate was off-the-record there was no transcript of the debate and the forum refused to release film of the event, there was a lengthy discussion about what exactly Jordan had said. At the *National Review Online*, Jim Geraghty said, "Why would Arab members of the audience come up and congratulate him for having the courage to speak the truth?"[22] At the *Captain's Quarters* blog, Edward Morrisey called on senators in Minnesota to hold a hearing regarding Jordan's comments "to establish once and for all whether the U.S. military has a policy of assassinating and torturing journalists in Iraq or anywhere else, and correct the terrible damage Mr. Jordan may have inflicted on our image abroad."[23]

In the face of the criticism, Jordan attempted to try and explain his remarks. In an interview, Jordan said that he and other executives had discussed with Pentagon officials the treatment of Iraqi journalists employed by American media who claim to have been tortured by the U.S. military. He said that the journalists had all made horrific statements about their treatment. Finally, in the face of the continuous pressure, on February 11, 2005, Jordan resigned saying, "I never meant to imply U.S. forces acted with ill intent when U.S. forces accidentally killed journalists, and I apologize to anyone who thought I said or believed otherwise."

Obviously, Jordan misspoke! The United States' military does not target journalists; however, there have been cases where American soldiers have displayed recklessness toward the media that borders on negligence. Jordan later sought to clarify and apologize for his initial comments, but, by then, it was too late. His initial comments generated a momentum of their own as they were discussed in conservative blogs and on talk shows. Magnified in this way, Jordan found it increasingly difficult to defend himself from the charge that he had slandered the United State's military.

In his resignation speech, Jordan said, he was leaving after 23 years "to prevent CNN from being unfairly tarnished by the controversy."[24] His words were an acceptance in the modern commercial world that journalists and media managers have to give thought to the damage done to their businesses—such pressures demand a blood sacrifice and realizing the threat to their value, media companies are loath to intervene on behalf of their employees.

Should Jordan have resigned? Perhaps in a different environment, Jordan would have survived, but the media environment during the Iraq war, and since the September 11 attacks, is a very different one to peacetime. The open space in which journalists work has been constricted, and the public is motivated by other currents of thought, such as patriotism and the need for unity.

Therefore, while to the naked eye the terrain looks very similar—the laws are the same, the society is the same—the reaction to various issues is totally different; in effect, the tolerance for dissent has evaporated. Journalists who fail to recognize this could expect little quarter, and, in this period, some lapsed into silence, rather than face an administration supported by the public and the conservative media.

Despite the passage of over 30 years, the Pentagon Papers case is still relevant. The legal decision set wartime administrations on a very different path than the one they might have followed. The all but total removal of prior restraint as a weapon against the media, forced administrations to rethink their policies towards the domestic media; as a result, it has resigned itself to an arm's length role, but in doing so, it has become far more sophisticated in the way it seeks to control news stories and events. Administrations have learnt that the blunt instrument of the law, and the attendant bad publicity, is not necessarily the best way to exercise control. Moreover, control can be best exercised by seeking to shape the environment in which journalists work by rallying the public and the conservative media to its side.

In essence, both in the lead-up to and during the Iraq war, the Bush administration fused its own views to the expression of patriotism in the United States. The result was Orwellian, but not unpredictable. In the same way that four legs were good and two legs were bad! Everything the Bush administration said was patriotic, while everything said by critics was unpatriotic and against the wishes of the American majority. This powerful combination had a considerable impact on journalists and others trying to exercise their right to freedom of expression.

Chapter 4

ALL QUIET ON THE HOME FRONT

Restriction on free thought and free speech is the most dangerous of all subversions. It is the one un-American act that could most easily defeat us.

—William O. Douglas, Supreme Court Justice

AL-JAZEERA'S PLUMMETING STOCK

Already condemned by the U.S. government for broadcasting pictures of dead and captured American soldiers in Iraq, the Arab satellite news service Al-Jazeera was to find itself at the center of a new controversy—this time on Wall Street.

The first indication of a problem came when freelancer Ammar al-Sankari arrived at the New York Stock Exchange (NYSE) on March 24, 2003 to record his daily business report for Al-Jazeera. After entering the NYSE, al-Sankari was led into a side office and asked to hand in his press credentials. He was told by officials "We are cutting back on broadcasting so you need to give us your badge and there won't be any more reporting for Al-Jazeera from the exchange."[1] Al-Sankari's freelance colleague, Ramzi Shiber, was also told to return his press badge.

In support of their decision, officials at the NYSE said that it was necessitated by the need to limit the number of media organizations working in the building. A spokesperson for the NYSE Ray Pellecchia tried to reinforce this impression when he said, "We've focused on those [broadcasters] who investors look to for business and financial news and unfortunately at this point that means we can't accommodate Al-Jazeera."[2] He was then quoted in newspapers as saying, "Over time we have had to limit the number of [reporters] broadcasting from here because of security precautions."[3] While these statements might have appeared reasonable to the American public, they were undermined by the fact that Al-Jazeera was the only media organization to be affected. The Qatar-based news organization had effectively been ejected from the floor of the world's largest stock exchange.

Although the NYSE dismissed claims that the ban was related to Al-Jazeera's broadcasting, there were media reports quoting unnamed sources who expressly linked pictures of U.S. servicemen to the ban. A *Los Angeles Times* article quoted an anonymous trader who said Al-Jazeera's credentials were revoked after a member of the exchange complained to officials.[4] While Pellecchia himself was quoted by the British *Financial Times* as saying only those providing "responsible business coverage" would be allowed to broadcast from within the exchange.[5]

Deeply concerned by the decision, Al-Jazeera turned to Nasdaq for permission to film business reports from its premises on Times Square. However, despite having used the facilities in the past, the broadcaster was met with a similar response, though one perhaps more explicit in tone. Nasdaq spokesperson Scott Peterson said, "In light of Al-Jazeera's recent conduct during the war, in which they have broadcast footage of U.S. POWs in alleged violation of the Geneva Convention[s], they are not welcome to broadcast from our facility at this time."[6] The media and press freedom organizations alike condemned the decision of the NYSE and Nasdaq.

A *New York Times* editorial on 30 March said the decision had placed "the princes of the free market" in the company of such countries as Jordan, Libya, and Tunisia who had all complained about Al-Jazeera's broadcasts in the past. Joel Simon, then acting director of the New York-based rights group the Committee to Protect Journalists (CPJ), said, "any effort by NYSE to prevent journalists from doing their jobs because of their news organization's editorial policy damages the NYSE's standing as a forum for the open exchange of news and information."[7] The Society of Professional Journalists (SPJ) also weighed in with the president-elect of the organization, Mac McKerral, saying that the decision "did nothing to support our country's image as a place where the free exchange of ideas and information serves as the foundation for everything America does."[8]

Faced by the mounting criticism, Nasdaq appeared to retreat from its earlier position. On March 27, the *New York Post* quoted Nasdaq spokesperson Silvia Davi who refused to support Peterson's earlier comments; instead, Davi would only admit that Al-Jazeera's request had been refused. "Beyond that, we can't comment," she said. During the early part of April, the NYSE entered into fresh discussions with Al-Jazeera about allowing the broadcaster back onto its trading floor. "They [Sankari and Shiber] are consultants to Al-Jazeera, [and] are two terrific young men who have reported from the floor of the exchange for two years," the Chairman and Chief Executive of the NYSE, Richard Grasso commented. Nearly one month after the initial discussions, in May, the two freelance business reporters were once again allowed to broadcast from the floor of the NYSE.

Irrespective of its eventual resolution, the incident involving Al-Jazeera reveals a number of troubling issues for media freedom and freedom of expression on the home front. Perhaps the most striking feature was the difference between home front violations and those committed on the battlefront. While those in the conflict zone centered on such issues as military and political censorship—the free flow of information, the reporting rules for journalists, and safety issues—the home front revealed a very different environment where the question of individual freedoms commingled with issues of patriotism and the right of the private sphere to determine its own actions and behavior. In this environment, if individual freedoms were to win the day, they would have to be victorious in a clash involving a number of competing tensions.

Moreover, while a violation might transparently be obvious in the conflict zone, there tended to be an absence of clarity in the violations on the home front. The question of whether there is a press freedom or freedom of expression issue in the dismissal of a journalist for protesting the war, an Internet Service Provider removing a website, the possible use of radio stations by their parent company to support the war, and the controversy over actors and singers protesting the war is often shrouded in ambiguity.

Moreover, it is an ambiguity that is reinforced when, as in the NYSE case, the offending company seeks to provide another reason for the violation such as "security," a failure to provide "responsible business reporting," or the lack of space in its offices. A further difficulty is the lack of protection under the First Amendment in some of these cases.

There is a common misunderstanding, even among some journalists, that the First Amendment provides blanket protection to both the media and individuals wishing to exercise freedom of expression. In fact, it merely acts as a limitation on "government," both federal and state;

preventing it from "abridging the freedom of speech, or of the press." The First Amendment does not, however, regulate the private sphere where many of the home front violations during the Second Gulf War took place. In consequence, a number of journalists faced difficulty in this new environment.

DISSENT: A DECIDEDLY UN-AMERICAN ACT

With the start of the Iraqi war, the public sought to express its support for the military. Due to the constrictions on dissent in this period, the media largely attempted to reflect the patriotic mood in the country, fearing, as with September 11, a backlash if they failed to do so. However, a number of journalists bravely refused to adhere to this policy of patriotism and attempted to provide their own dissenting viewpoints.

Furthermore, there were other journalists who felt unable to separate their profession from their own feelings and decided to protest the war. This led to them attending anti-war rallies or practicing civil disobedience. If the reporters believed that their media organizations would support the exercise of their civil rights, they were mistaken.

In San Francisco, technology journalist Henry Norr of the *San Francisco Chronicle* was dismissed from his job for protesting the war. Planning to attend an anti-war rally with his wife and daughter in the Bay area, Norr informed his employers that he fully expected to be arrested as a result of his attending the demonstration and would not be coming to the office on that day. On March 19, Norr was arrested by police for blocking traffic and was held in custody for several hours. Later, Norr was informed that he would be unable to write for the *Chronicle* and that he was being suspended without pay for falsifying a time card.

According to Norr, when he returned to work after his arrest, he filled out his time card to show that his day of demonstrating was a sick day. Norr said he did this because "I was feeling nauseated by the lies and the arrogance and the racism. I was feeling depressed. All kinds of reasons. And, of course, by the time work started, I was in a lot of pain because the cop had twisted my arm in trying to get me to move."[9] Norr went on to claim that the time card was a pretext and that the real reason for his suspension and subsequent dismissal was his anti-war stance. There was also a disagreement over the newspaper's policy towards employees participating in protests.

Speaking in an interview with the *Democracy Now!* website, Norr said that the original policy had been negotiated in 2002, but, after Norr's participation in a protest, a memorandum was sent to all *Chronicle* staff stating that they were to obtain the permission of their editor before marching. Norr said the policy existed for several days before a second memorandum introduced a complete ban on staff protesting.[10] In Texas, the experiences of Brent Flynn would be similar to that of Norr's.

Flynn, a reporter and columnist for the Star Community Newspaper group—the Dallas Fort-Worth branch of the American Community Newspaper chain—whose columns often appeared in the *Lewsiville Leader* attended an anti-war march in Lewisville. In his last column for the *Lewsiville Leader* he mentioned his participation in a protest march and criticized the right-wing movement that sees the "mass demonstrations of democracy as a threat to the country, not as a show of its strength." Flynn then said, "These useful idiots . . . would not recognize true democracy if it marched past their front door on the way to the voting booth."[11]

As a result, the editor of the *Lewisville Leader* decided to remove Flynn from his duties as a columnist while retaining him as a journalist. His salary was not reduced as a consequence. Commenting on the decision, Flynn wrote on his personal website, www.brentflynn.com, "I am convinced that if my column was supportive of the war and it was a pro-war rally that I attended, they would not have dared cancel my column . . . . The fact that the column was cancelled just days before the start of the U.S. invasion of Iraq raises serious questions about the motives of the cancellation."[12]

While Flynn and Norr found themselves disciplined for combining their media work with dissent, Kurt Hauglie's column was rejected due to its anti-war stance. After writing a column for his newspaper the *Huron Daily Tribune* that criticized the war, Hauglie was told by the editor that she was worried that it would upset the newspaper's readership. He was then told that the column might be included at a later date; however, after two weeks the journalists was told that it would never be printed. Finally, on March 25, Hauglie decided to resign in protest at the failure to print his column.

The incidents involving Flynn, Hauglie, and Norr reveal the difficulty of swimming against the current in the United States during wartime. Although it is true that the United States can be justly proud of its record on civil and political rights, the impulse to censor dissent during conflict and the descent into patriotic rhetoric are not the sole preserve of governments. What these cases reveal is the impact that such movements of opinion have on the media; in particular, it shows that while there is apparent lip service to such fundamental rights as free speech, an overriding concern is the impact that dissent will have on the readership or viewers or listeners of a media organization.

Seen from another perspective, there is also an ethical dimension to the debate, namely whether journalists are capable of jointly having a public sphere, where they carry out their profession in an unbiased and objective manner, and a private sphere, where they have the right to dissent. Media professionals are split on this issue with some journalists and editors saying they do not vote out of fear of bias, while others believe that like many other professions they are capable of separating their private life from their public life. Fundamental to the discussion is the right of individual choice and it is noticeable in the cases of Flynn and Norr that this was removed by their respective newspapers. It is also worth noting that in Norr's case the *Chronicle*, echoing the actions of the NYSE in the Al-Jazeera case, subscribed its actions to another cause: the time card.

In Hauglie's case, which involved a very real act of censorship, the newspaper changed its approach at the onset of war. The Michigan journalist had written other dissenting columns before the war, but once the U.S. military forces engaged with those of the Iraqi's it was felt that criticism would upset the readership. As such, these were the actions of a newspaper altering its approach in order to stay in lockstep with public opinion and a depressing sign that the media were straying further and further away from the 1960s and 1970s when the media led criticism of the Vietnam War.

The closure of the Yellowtimes.org also showed a fear of public opinion. Having outraged both the Pentagon and the public with pictures of U.S. fatalities and prisoners of war taken from the Al-Jazeera satellite broadcaster, the alternative Internet news site Yellowtimes.org found itself briefly closed down on Sunday March 23, 2003. On the following day, the Web hosting company Vortech Hosting closed down the offending website indefinitely.

According to Yellowtimes.org's editor Erich Marquardt, the news service was told that the photos of U.S. soldiers amounted to adult or graphic content and it was in breach of its terms-of-use contractual agreement that gives the host a wide discretion when defining adult content.[13] Commenting on the decision of Vortech Hosting, Marquardt said, "They own the servers and they can decide what goes on them."[14] Responding to media criticism, Vortech Hosting said in an e-mail, "We understand free press and all but we don't want someone's family member to see them on some site. It is disrespectful, tacky, and disgusting."[15]

In the following days there were unsubstantiated rumors in *Florida Today* that a local supermarket had briefly removed from sale copies of *USA Today* featuring a front page showing a dead U.S. soldier. The decision was at the apparent behest of customers who had complained about the image—the newspapers were later returned to the shelves. Moreover, the debate over the images on the Internet, and in other media, became intertwined with a discussion over whether it was right and proper to show such images. It is a debate that stretches back to World War II.

During World War II there had been a general prohibition on images of dead U.S. soldiers. However, toward the end of the war President Roosevelt gave his permission for the release of film and photographs of soldiers killed in the hard fought Pacific campaign. Instead of upsetting the public, as some thought, the images had the effect of rallying public support for the war. The question of whether certain images were suitable for consumption also arose after the September 11 attacks on the World Trade Center and the Pentagon.

On the day of the September 11 attacks, with the Twin Towers burning, many news outlets filming the tragedy live chose to show the images of people forced to jump from the buildings. The images were also shown the next day in various newspapers around the world as a means of portraying the full horror of the attacks. Such images were heavily criticized because it was claimed that relatives could identify the victims. Arguments over this type of reporting were exacerbated some months later by the decision of a number of broadcasters and websites to show parts of a video displaying the execution of *Wall Street Journal* reporter Daniel Pearl by Muslim extremists in Pakistan.

After the video of Pearl's death became available, a number of media organizations made the decision to place it on the Internet. Out of concern for his relatives, the Federal Bureau of Investigation (FBI) invited Ogrish.com and its host Pro Hosters to remove the video. The request was extra-legal and without the force of the courts and initially the host complied, only to later reverse its decision. In addition to Ogrish.com, a Boston weekly, the *Phoenix*, also placed a link on its website to the Pearl Video. Seeking to justify itself, a *Phoenix* editorial said, "If there is anything that should galvanize every non-Jew hater in the world... against the perpetrators and supporters of those who committed this unspeakable murder, it should be viewing this video."[16]

Caught between the rights of the media, on the one side, and the sheer horror of the images on the other, there is blame to be apportioned on both sides. While the media has an important duty to inform the public, it is difficult to escape the feeling that the pictures of an execution or of people jumping from a burning building are gratuitous in the extreme and meant for the sheer titillation of viewers. However, it is possible to separate these examples from those where there is a genuine need to show graphic images to the public and this separation revolves on the question of "newsworthiness."

In an age where military press officers spend much of their time describing war as a series of clean, surgical strikes against a largely unseen enemy, the pictures of dead soldiers, from whichever side, tell the true story—while it may be possible to ignore these images it is impossible to deny that this is the reality of war. As a result, the media has a right to show these images to the public. Setting aside this issue, perhaps the true issue in the Yellowtimes.org case is whether or not it amounts to censorship.

Unfortunately, while the removal of Yellowtimes.org appears to be censorship in its truest sense, as previously discussed, it falls outside the ambit of the First Amendment. Instead, it is merely a question of the contractual relationship between the website and the host. Based on the view of some legal experts, the host by appearing to exercise "editorial control" is in danger of losing its own protection against possible third-party actions against the website itself, but this does not answer the fundamental question of whether a host should be allowed to interfere with content where such content is not expressly illegal? Furthermore, should the host be able to justify censorship in the name of "good taste?"

At present, the questions are far from being answered and have tended to become obscured in the overall noise of the war. One possible answer might be to create voluntary bodies that review complaints involving issues such as those in the Yellowtimes.org case. The body would operate along the lines of a European style press council functioning independently of government and made up of industry figures. Alternatively, disputes could be resolved by the creation of an ombudsman for website hosts who would be tasked with the duty of judging whether the complaints of the individual websites could be upheld.

Although it is not entirely clear whether such procedures would work, it is important to realize that at present there is little protection for a website against the accusation that it is depicting adult content rather than a newsworthy item. Because of this, in the clash between hosts and websites over questions of news and censorship, the principles of media freedom are coming a very poor second to commercial considerations.

In many of the cases the urge to "rally around the flag" played a significant role in forcing censorship on various media outlets. Coupled to this was the ability of actors in the private sphere to stem criticism by claiming that the act was committed for an entirely different reason; in the case of Al-Jazeera it was a question of space, with Norr it was his time card, and with Yellowtimes.org a question of simple decency. All of these actions were outside the sphere of government influence and yet all of them reflected the Bush administration's belief that in the time of war dissent was to be silenced; for this reason they provide a powerful lesson about the reach of the federal government.

The relationship of radio owner Clear Channel to pro-war rallies was also another example of the ability of the federal government to refrain from direct involvement while continuing to shape the "censorial environment."

"DARKENED SELF-INTEREST": FLYING THE FLAG AND RALLYING BEHIND THE WAR

Writing in *The Nation* on June 2, Alisa Solomon said, "From shopping malls to cyberspace, Hollywood to the Ivy League, Americans have taken it upon themselves to stifle and shame those who question the legitimacy of the war on Iraq."[17] Solomon's statement captured the mood at the time perfectly—with the ongoing war in Iraq, and with the previous statements on dissent by officials such as Ashcroft and Fleischer continuing to pervade the air, Americans from all walks of life were voicing their anger toward dissenters. In effect, as Anthony Romero, executive director of the American Civil Liberties Union (ACLU) pointed out, the remarks of government officials were a "license" to "shut-down alternative views."[18]

The prevailing environment could perhaps be best summed up by a single expression of President Bush who said in the aftermath of the September 11 attacks, "Either you are with us or you are with the terrorists."[19] It was a choice that did not go unnoticed at some commercial radio stations, particularly at the stations owned by the San Antonio-based Clear Channel.

On March 26, the *International Herald Tribune* published an editorial titled, "Behind Pro War Protests, a Company with Ties to Bush," by Paul Krugman which looked at the way some radio stations were showing support for the war and examining the apparent relationship between Clear Channel and President Bush.[20]

According to the editorial, which was originally published in the *New York Times*, the vice-chairman of Clear Channel, Tom Hicks, was chairman of the University of Texas Investment Management Company—UTIMCO—when President Bush was governor of Texas. Moreover, chairman of Clear Channel, Lowry Mays, was also on the board of UTIMCO. In 1998, Hicks purchased the Texas Rangers in a business arrangement that apparently "made Bush a multimillionaire." The implication of the editorial was that, with ownership of almost 50 percent of all radio stations in the United States, Clear Channel was not only influencing the play list of its radio stations, but also orchestrating pro-war support for President Bush.

The basis for these accusations was a series of rallies around the United States. Organized by Glenn Beck, a talk-show host with a syndicated radio program for Premier Radio Networks, which is owned by Clear Channel, the "Rallies for America" were a series of meetings for those who wished to support the soldiers in Iraq. Held in Atlanta, Cleveland, San Antonio, and Cincinnati as well as other cities, the rallies were attended by as many as 20,000 people wishing to declare their support.

Speaking on behalf of Clear Channel, Lisa Dollinger said that the rallies were not organized or orchestrated by Clear Channel's headquarters. "Any rallies that our stations have been a part of have been of their own initiative and in response to the expressed desires of their listeners and communities."[21] On the question of the reason for the rallies Dollinger said, "They're not intended to be pro-military. It's more of a thank you to the troops. They're just patriotic rallies."[22]

Despite the fact that there is no evidence to suggest that the rallies were organized by the San Antonio headquarters of Clear Channel, it appeared strange that a spokesperson would, after stating there was no connection, then go on to say what the rallies were actually for. This is perhaps one of the most troubling aspects of the "Rallies for America," while not organized by Clear Channel, they were certainly condoned if not supported by headquarters and this raises a number of questions for radio stations.

As Glen Robinson, a law professor and former Commissioner of the Federal Communications Commission (FCC) commented, "I can't say it violates any of a broadcaster's obligations, but it sounds like a borderline manufacturing of the news."[23] In Clear Channel's case, the accusation is well founded because the company owns stations that provide news and its syndicates are in effect also creating the news thereby causing a conflict of interest. Furthermore, the repeal of the "Fairness Doctrine" in

1987, requiring broadcasters to offer "balanced news" allows radio stations to become involved in community-based activities, which might have been prevented prior to 1987.

The net result was that a media company with links to the Republican party and President Bush allowed its radio stations to pursue a policy of support for the military and the war in Iraq. By doing so, it inflamed public opinion and managed to cow dissenters such as Natalie Maines of the Country and Western band the Dixie Chicks, who was forced to apologize for comments made at a concert in London, England. It was yet another case of the commercial field carrying out the work of the federal government at "arms length."

Speaking of the accusations that this was a clever plot to undermine the critics of the war, Jenny Toomey, the executive director of the Future of Music Coalition, said, "This is just enlightened self-interest in some ways or darkened self-interest."[24] It just so happened that the self-interest mirrored that of the Bush administration.

"HOORAY FOR HOLLYWOOD": THE CLIMATE OF FEAR AND THE ANTI-WAR CELEBRITIES

In the April 12 edition of *TV Guide*, the head of the movies and mini-series division of the Canadian production company Alliance Atlantis, Ed Gernon, made a comparison between the current mini-series he was working on, "Hitler: The Rise of Evil" and the War in Iraq. With regard to the Bush administration's pre-emptive strike and its acceptance by the public, Gernon said there was a similar "fearful acceptance" behind Germany's acceptance of Adolf Hitler. Gernon was also quoted as saying, "[the mini-series on Hitler] is basically down to an entire nation gripped by fear, who ultimately chose to give up their civil rights and plunged the whole world into war." He then said, "I can't think of a better time to examine this history than now."[25]

A pre-publication copy of Gernon's interview was handed to the *New York Post*, along with *TV Guide*, which is owned by Rupert Murdoch. Comment on his interview appeared on the *New York Post's* notorious Page 6 under the heading "Rise of Lunacy at CBS" which predicted, "The scraping sound you hear next month will be Hollywood's anti-Americanism hitting bottom with the CBS movie "Hitler: The Rise of Evil." The article also carried a disclaimer from CBS president Leslie Moonves who did not accept the apparent parallel between Hitler and President Bush. [26]

On April 9, John Podhoretz in another *New York Post* article commented that CBS "just devoted millions of dollars and will devote four hours of prime time to the mini-series dedicated to the Bush = Hitler proposition." Later in the article, Podhoretz attacked CBS, "What they commissioned, it appears, is an act of slander against the president of the United States—and by extension, toward the United States itself."[27]

With the conservative media mobilized, the pressure on Gernon had begun to build. CBS was the first to publicly dissociate itself from the producer's words when it said, "We found Mr. Gernon's comments in the *TV Guide* to be insensitive and outright wrong." Wishing to protect its film product, CBS then went on to say, "It is very important that viewers understand that these views are not reflected in the tone or the content of the mini-series . . . "[28] In its April 11 article, "Producer is a Casualty in CBS's 'Hitler Mini-series,' " The *Washington Post* announced Gernon had been fired.

The most worrying aspect of Gernon's case is the sheer speed with which he was convicted in the public arena. No sooner had Gernon given the interview, a copy of the speech was disseminated to journalists who attacked him. Essentially, Gernon had given his interview, been attacked in the media, and dismissed before the article had even been published! The producer's dismissal was yet another sign of the climate of fear that existed among the media profession who feared losing their own jobs if they spoke out. This atmosphere prompted the Screen Actor's Guild (SAG) to liken it to McCarthyism and state "even the hint of the blacklist must never be tolerated."[29]

Aside from Gernon's plight, the actions of *The New York Post*, CBS and Alliance Atlantis are also worth noting. In essence, Page 6 and Podhoretz's article tilted CBS and Alliance Atlantis into dismissing the producer. It was a classic example of a company in wartime forced to make a choice between the defense of an employee and the defense of a product. Given the reason for the existence of companies, namely profit and commercial success, it was not hard to see which way the companies were going to jump.

If CBS and Alliance Atlantis were in any doubt, Page 6 makes it clear what would happen with its reference to the "sound" of "Hollywood's anti-Americanism hitting bottom." In other words, CBS was to be identified with Gernon's words and the result would be low viewing figures for its expensive "mini-series." Podhoretz's article reinforces this message by playing the patriotism card and alluding to a "slander" of both the "president" and "the United States" and, by virtue of this, the American people.

Within Hollywood itself the question of profit, fears over the success of a film product, and the question of patriotism were all to play a role in many of the incidents involving actors and actresses who wished to express themselves on the issue of the Iraq war. This was particularly true of *West Wing* star Martin Sheen.

An outspoken liberal for many years, Martin Sheen took every opportunity to protest the Iraq war causing him on one anti-war march to cover his mouth in duct tape in a biting criticism of those who wished to prevent his exercise of dissent. Sheen also angered many members of the public by appearing in a commercial that called for more time to be given to the United Nations' Weapons Inspectors in their search for nuclear and biological weapons. As a result, he received hate mail, and NBC, the television broadcaster carrying the *West Wing*, received mail inviting them to sack him. At www.celiberal.com, where supporters were asked to boycott the actor's work, one protestor wrote, "Martin Sheen is not my president. George W. Bush is."[30] Sheen's defiant stand and the criticism he received were to have an impact on his relationship with NBC.

In early March 2003, Sheen told the *Los Angeles Times* that the *West Wing's* staff had been "100 percent supportive but top network executives let it be known they're 'very uncomfortable' with where I'm at on the war."[31] However, Sheen's comments were rebutted by an NBC spokesperson, who said the executives respected his personal views on the war. Sean Penn was also to lose out financially as the result of fears over whether his anti-war views would harm a film project.

Having gone further than other Hollywood stars and made the decision to visit Iraq in mid-December 2002, Sean Penn subsequently made a number of appearances on television. After a January appearance on the CNN's *Larry King Show*, he received a telephone call from Hollywood producer Steve Bing who was to produce Penn in a movie called, *Why Men Shouldn't Marry*. During the telephone conversation, Bing apparently asked for an assurance that he would not speak politically. Penn refused to provide such a guarantee claiming that it breached his civil rights. He was later dismissed from the film project and Penn claimed that a Hollywood blacklist was in operation.

Commenting on the possibility of a blacklist, Sherry Bebitch Jeffe of the University of Southern California said, "I think there really isn't a formal blacklist, but there probably is some caution on the part of the business end of Hollywood about using a star in a multi-million dollar movie when there is a risk that there might be a boycott of the star."[32]

For film couple Tim Robbins and Susan Sarandon, their vocal criticism of the war also led to the cancellation of appearances. Asked to appear at a tribute to the fifteenth anniversary of the film in which they both starred *Bull Durham*, the two actors were subsequently told not to attend the Baseball Hall of Fame where the tribute was to be held. Speaking of the decision, President of the Hall Dale Petroskey said, "with our troops committed in Iraq—a strong possibility existed that they would have used the Hall of Fame as a backdrop for their views."

In a letter to Robbins, Petroskey, a former assistant press secretary under President Reagan, wrote, "We believe your very public criticism of President Bush at this important—and sensitive—time in our nation's history helps undermine the U.S. position, which ultimately could put our troops in even more danger. As an institution, we stand behind our President and our troops in this conflict."[33] Petroskey failed to elaborate on exactly why a speech by Robbins would "undermine" and "ultimately" endanger the troops in Iraq!

Sarandon also faced similar treatment at the hands of the United Way Group of Tampa Bay who had invited the actress to be the keynote speaker at an April 11 event paid for by the United Way women's group. According to the *St. Petersburg Times*, Sarandon's brother Terry Tomalin, who works for the *Times*, had asked her to speak.[34] Chairwoman of the group, Robin Carson was worried that the organization would be seen as a platform for Sarandon's political views. "We had a strong mission for that day, and we felt that there was a potential that we would create divisiveness in the community, where our mission was to unite the community." Sarandon's speaking fees were to have been paid by the St. Petersburg Times Fund.

On April 15, Robbins spoke at the National Press Club in Washington, DC. During the speech, when commenting on his recent experiences, he said democracy had been "compromised by fear and hatred" and that a "climate of fear" existed in the United States.[35] With film companies seeking to protect film projects and their relationship with the public rather than upholding freedom of speech, Robbins aptly summed up the Hollywood environment.

With its preference for placing the success of its film projects ahead of free expression, Hollywood film companies were being shortsighted. By failing to support actors who wished to protest the war, companies were ignoring the future possibility that censorship would be applied to their film products. Although they may have felt they were forestalling this day by supporting the federal government, the acceptance of censorship in one area might well make it more acceptable in others.

On the issue of blacklisting, though, there was no evidence of this in the Hollywood of the twenty-first century. However, the experiences of actors such as Sheen, Sarandon, and Penn were indicative of an underlying censorship founded on a desire not to be seen out of step with the public. Confronted by a patriotic public and Bush administration, film and television broadcasters hunkered down and kept their own counsel rather than supporting actors like Sheen, who faced hate mail, or Janeane Garofalo, who faced a campaign to remove her from a television project.

Outside of Hollywood, there was a debate in the media over whether celebrities had a right to espouse their political views. Many critics viewed the criticism voiced by celebrities to be an abuse of their relationship with the media because they were unloading a personal viewpoint on the unsuspecting public. However, this failed to acknowledge the right of celebrities to express their own personal opinions, and attempted to apply a hypocritical rule that said it is acceptable for celebrities to be interviewed on a myriad of other subjects for which they may or may not be suitable just so long as it is not about the present conflict. As a result, there was a double standard at play with certain individuals claiming the right to decide the limits of free speech for others.

THE IRAQ WAR AND THE RESCISSION OF THE RIGHT TO FREE SPEECH

In answer to a question on the right to hold terrorists, Supreme Court Justice Antonin Scalia replied that "the Constitution just sets minimums," and "Most of the rights you enjoy go way beyond what the Constitution requires."[36] Aside from sparking a lively debate on the nature of the Constitution, Scalia's words also served to show that since September 11 a number of pivotal rights Americans believed to be fundamental— such as *habeas corpus*—were slowly being eroded in the name of the War against Terrorism.

Significantly, the judge's opinion exposed one of the fundamental problems for dissenters on the home front during the Iraq war. Although there was a continued focus on the question of whether Constitutional rights were being upheld, home front censorship, which was reliant on various forms of pressure, was either being ignored or misunderstood. While fears over censorship led to criticism of Internet Service Providers (ISPs), the

NYSE, the owners of media organizations, film producers, or the president of the Baseball Hall of Fame, there was a general failure to question the environment in which these individuals and organizations were acting. This failure to inquire, to investigate, created the loophole through which the Bush administration could escape blame for any of the home front violations.

Therefore, with efforts being concentrated on the erosion of Constitutional rights, it was easy to overlook the Bush administration's double standards on the issue of free speech. A double standard that can clearly be seen in the behavior of the administration over the issue of the boycott of French goods.

When answering a question on the boycott of French goods posed at one of his daily press conferences, then presidential spokesperson Ari Fleischer said, "I think you are seeing the American people speak spontaneously. And that is right." Later he said, "It is the right of people in Europe to speak their mind. So, too, is it the right of the American people to speak theirs."[37] But the subtext of Fleischer's words were that the American people had the right of free speech only on issues which supported the Bush administration. When it came to criticizing the Bush administration or offering dissent on the decision to go to war in Iraq, these individuals were not to be afforded those same rights. Using this policy as a foundation, the Bush administration has been able to use the public's patriotism to "tilt" the commercial sphere into reinforcing this message.

For this reason, the environment in which both the media and dissenters found themselves was totally removed from that of previous conflicts. The pull and push of patriotism, the innate conservatism of business, and the lack of protection under the First Amendment all played a part in reinforcing the right of the federal government to dictate how individuals exercise their rights to free speech and free expression.

Due to these movements, not only were there more potential violations, but there was also an attendant ambiguity that came with the violations—an ambiguity that made it harder to expose the problem. From the Bush administration: "reminders to all Americans that they need to watch what they say, watch what they do," to the enraged public: "Martin Sheen is not my president. George W. Bush is," to business: "It is very important that viewers understand that these views are not reflected in the tone or the content of the mini-series," there were links and connections in the cycle, but they were exceedingly difficult to prove. Nonetheless, the results were always the same: journalists, film producers, and celebrities, all found their right to free expression curtailed.

Occurring after the start of the war, the military's request to CBS to delay the broadcasting of photographs depicting the humiliation and torture of inmates at the Abu Ghraib prison provides a stark example of how an administration can influence the media and yet remain at arm's length.

Chapter 5

THE PRISON, THE GENERAL, AND THE FLEXIBLE BROADCASTER

This was not to suppress anything. What I asked CBS News to do was to delay the release of the pictures, given the current situation in Iraq, which was as bad as it had been since major combat ended, because I thought it [would] bring direct harm to our troops; it would kill our troops.

—Chairman of the Joint Chiefs of Staff, General Richard Myers

A QUESTION OF ATTRIBUTION?

On July 22, 2003 the U.S. army finally caught up with Saddam Hussein's two sons, Uday and Qusay. Following information provided by an Iraqi civilian, the 101st Airborne Division carried out an operation in northeast Mosul that saw them cordon off a residence where the two brothers were believed to be staying. When attempting to enter the property, the soldiers were met with gunfire, injuring three soldiers. Having safely evacuated the injured soldiers, the ground commanders used heavier weapons and a number of rockets were fired into the house. With these having failed to dislodge the second-floor occupants, ten tube-launched missiles were fired at the house.

According to the head of U.S. military operations in Iraq, Army Lieutenant General Ricardo Sanchez, who gave a press conference in Baghdad, it was believed that at this point both Uday and Qusay were killed. Another occupant of the house was killed when soldiers later entered the building. Once the bodies of Saddam Hussein's sons had been retrieved, the military sought to confirm their identity by approaching "four separate senior members of the regime ... including ... Abid Hamid Mahmud, Saddam Hussein's personal secretary."[1]

In addition, x-rays were studied showing old wounds suffered by Uday in a previous assassination attempt, as well as dental records showing a 90 percent match for Uday and 100 percent match for Qusay. During his press conference, Sanchez said the failure to match Uday's dental records with 100 percent accuracy was entirely due to damage to the body suffered during the firefight.

Two days after their deaths, the Coalition Provisional Authority decided to release photographs of Uday and Qusay. The photographs were released initially in Baghdad, but later found their way to all of the major media organizations. Describing the way in which the photographs were released, Elie Harb, assistant editor-in-chief of the Lebanese Broadcasting Company (LBC), said, "The situation was very strange ... when they [the U.S. military] permitted all the film crews to enter, it was a small tent with two bodies. You had to shoot close-ups ... of disgusting un-humanitarian shots. We were obliged to show them. There are always exceptions."[2]

Responding to reporter's questions about the decision to release the pictures, U.S. Defense Secretary Donald Rumsfeld said the pictures' dissemination was the right decision. "These two individuals [Uday and Qusay] are particularly vicious individuals. They are dead now. We know that. They have been carefully identified. The Iraqi people have been waiting for confirmation of that and they, in my view, deserve having confirmation of that," Rumsfeld said.[3]

In reply to another reporter, who compared the photos to the Bush administration's vociferous objections to photos of dead American soldiers previously shown on the Middle Eastern broadcaster Al-Jazeera, Rumsfeld commented:

> The more I thought about the importance of having the Iraqi people gain conviction that that crowd [the Hussein regime] is through, and the fact that it could reduce the number of Americans and coalition people who might be killed, and it could increase the number of people who will come forward with information and give us intelligence as to where the remainder of these people are, and where conceivably it'll reduce the number of recruits and jihadists coming into the country because they'll find it's a less hospitable environment than they might have thought, that seems to me to outweigh the sensitivities.[4]

Within the media there was a wide-ranging debate about the use of the photographs with some media supporting their use while others called for the need for those killed in war to be shown dignity. A *New York Post* editorial on July 25, 2003, said, "[T] he release—while contrary to normal Pentagon practice—was a good idea,"[5] and a *Dallas Morning News* editorial went further saying, "[B] eing unable to discern the basic ethical difference between leaders of a terrorist police state and American GIs there to overthrow them betrays a troubling moral relativism. Americans are the good guys, remember?"[6]

Those who disagreed with the publication of the photographs often focused on the hypocrisy displayed by the allies when pictures of dead allied soldiers were shown on Arab television. "Isn't there a hint of distasteful triumphalism in exhibiting vanquished enemies as trophies, in a way reminiscent of medieval barbarism? Britain and the US were rightly shocked when an Arab television station broadcast film of dead Americans during the war. The US is a great democracy that has so much to offer the world, but by reducing herself to the level of her enemies she loses moral supremacy," trumpeted the conservative but anti-war British newspaper, the *Daily Mail*.[7]

Perhaps one of the best critiques of the decision came from Germany. Commenting on the photographs, the *Frankfurter Rundschau* said, "We're talking about human dignity." The paper went on to say, "Independent of the crimes Uday and Qusay were accused of, the display represents a violation of the basic principles of the civilized world."[8]

Aside from the moral implications of the pictures, themselves, editors of newspapers and television broadcasters also had to decide how, if they were to show them, the pictures were to be presented. Although many took the decision to show the pictures, many media organizations were fearful of upsetting their audiences and so went to great lengths to prepare viewers and readers for the shock of the photographs. However, on the whole, the American media believed that the pictures were worthy of display.

Speaking for many, Jerry Nachman, MSNBC's editor-in-chief described the situation in the following manner, "If it's the biggest story in the world today, how do we not cover it. . . . If it's television, how do we not air it."[9] Accepting this view, the cable channels— CNN, Fox News Channel, and MSNBC—continually displayed the pictures on their news programs, as did the terrestrial channels, ABC, CBS, and NBC.

Some newspapers, however, opted to deal with the photographs in a manner that shielded their readers from the goriness. This, in turn, called for a degree of circumspection.

For instance, at *USA Today*, editors said they had decided to use a photo on page one that showed someone looking at the photos as they were shown on television. The newspaper then went inside with a short article about the decision to show the pictures, alongside the actual photographs. "Obviously the photographs are repulsive, but just as obviously the reader won't be able to judge the story or the [U.S.] government's decision to release them unless they're published," commented Brian Gallagher, the executive editor at the newspaper.[10] "It came down to newsworthiness," said Kevin Courtney, speaking on behalf of the *South Florida Sun-Sentinel*. "We put up a warning [on the website] advising users that it had graphic content. The decision was based on newsworthiness."[11]

Obviously, once the photographs had been released, it was difficult for the media to avoid publishing them—the genie was out of the bottle! Courtney's comments were correct: the photographs were extremely newsworthy because they showed a vital element of the war in Iraq; moreover, as was said, for the public to assess the correctness of the Bush administration's decision to release the pictures, it was necessary to at least see them.

The Bush administration's reasoning was, however, less sure. According to Defense Secretary Rumsfeld, the pictures were shown to convince the Iraqi public that the two brothers were dead and it was a means of lowering morale among the insurgents. But, such a view failed to entertain the notion that the pictures of the dead brothers might inflame tensions in the country and lead to more jihadist recruits and further acts of violence. The problem with the Bush administration's assessment was that it appeared to be made on very little factual information. How could the Bush administration, or even Defense Secretary Rumsfeld really know that the pictures would reduce the number of fighters or encourage others to come forward to provide information on the insurgents?

Moreover, there appeared to be a misunderstanding about the nature of the forces ranged against the allies in Iraq. Defense Secretary Rumsfeld's comments appeared to imply that much of the fighting was with the remnants of the former regime, but, in fact, the fighting at that time was being conducted by a mixture of die-hard Baathists and jihadists who had entered the country to fight the allies. Given this fact, why would the death of two sons of the country's former secular ruler make a difference? In fact, if anything, the opposite was true, the pictures would increase the number of fighters because it showed Muslims defiled by Westerners. Rather than working for them, the pictures were anti-western propaganda undermining allied attempts to introduce democracy and stability to Iraq.

As Lawrence M. Hinman of the *San Diego Union-Tribune* said on July 25, "The public display of the bodies of the Hussein sons will serve to inflame already enraged feelings throughout the Middle East and will, in all probability, lead to further guerilla attacks.[12] A member of the public writing to Reuter's editors said, "Have you not learned from [the Hollywood film] *Black Hawk Down*? Parading deceased Americans in the streets of Mogadishu? Are you not repeating this mistake?"[13]

The writer was alluding to the televised scenes of a dead U.S. soldier being dragged through the streets of Mogadishu by militiamen, but there have been other situations where the Bush administration has made formal complaints about the use of such imagery. Interestingly, the U.S. military had grave reservations about the use of the pictures for precisely this reason: namely, the loss of their ability to criticize the media for using imagery of U.S. soldiers.

Regarding the media, commentators were right. Once the military had allowed the pictures to be taken, news broadcasters and publishers had legitimate reasons for telling the story and showing the pictures. In effect, they were news.

The problem came with the rules that were being laid down by the administration on this subject. Later, in the heated discussion over the use of the photos showing torture and inhumane treatment at Abu Ghraib prison, the Bush administration would find it difficult to make the same arguments. After all, if the pictures of Saddam Hussein's dead sons were newsworthy, so were the pictures showing U.S. soldiers humiliating their prisoners.

Unlike the pictures of the dead Hussein brothers, the media would also have difficulties with the Abu Ghraib pictures. In the case of Uday and Qusay, the pictures were released for the purposes of verification and as a means of lowering the morale of the insurgents; in the Abu Ghraib case, the opposite would be argued by the military to the media. The release of pictures showing American soldiers treating Iraqi's inhumanely would further inflame tensions and lead to further deaths of U.S. soldiers.

The result was confusion—when do you release pictures, and when do you withhold them? It seemed the only real logic to the situation was that the Bush administration felt able to move the goalposts whenever it so desired.

Fortunately, when there was a need to prevent disclosure, the Bush administration was able to strong-arm a malleable and pliable news broadcaster into agreeing to withhold the pictures for nearly two weeks. The case is not only one of the best examples of indirect pressure against journalists, it is perhaps the purest example of how an administration can influence the media without resorting to legal action. It is the very definition of the arm's length principle. Sadly, the news broadcaster in question was CBS, historically, one of the most independent terrestrial television broadcasters in the United States.

"TWO WEEKS AGO 60 MINUTES II RECEIVED AN APPEAL"

With the story of torture at Abu Ghraib, the media were always three steps behind the Bush administration. Starting in late 2002, there were articles in the media and stories circulating among journalists that the Central Intelligence Agency (CIA) was apparently using "strong-arm" practices when interrogating captured prisoners in Afghanistan. Such stories were followed in the early part of 2003 with news that the Bush administration had accepted that these practices were necessary in the war against terrorism. During late 2003, the Associated Press (AP) published a story stating that prisoners in the Abu Ghraib prison in Iraq were being abused.

Despite the existence of these stories, and in particular, the AP story, the mainstream media failed to focus on the story. They allowed it to simply slide and there were few editors who realized the importance of, and had the resources to follow up the stories because they were already overstretched covering the ongoing insurrection in Iraq.

Another problem was that the Bush administration remained extremely quiet on the issue of the abuse and sought to downplay its importance. An example of this came on January 16, 2004, when the U.S. military in Baghdad issued a press release. The press release said simply, "An investigation has been initiated into reported incidents of detainee abuse at a coalition forces detention facility. The release of specific information concerning the incidents could hinder the investigation, which is in its early stages. The investigation will be conducted in a thorough and professional manner."[14]

Phrased in neutral terms, the press release was innocuous and it failed to ignite much interest among the mainstream media. Those who did cover the story placed it inside their newspaper and not on the front page. After that, according to Sherry Ricchiardi who examined the issue of why the media failed to report the Abu Ghraib story for the *American Journalism Review*, the "story largely disappeared."[15]

What the press release did not say was that a number of American prison guards had terrorized, humiliated, and in some cases tortured a number of prisoners at Abu Ghraib. The disturbing treatment of the prisoners was uncovered after a major investigation into the detention center ordered by Lieutenant General Ricardo S. Sanchez.

In its 53 pages, the report, written by Major General Antonio M. Taguba, catalogued a series of abuses including:

> Breaking chemical lights and pouring the phosphoric liquid on detainees; pouring cold water on naked detainees; beating detainees with a broom handle and a chair; threatening male detainees with rape; allowing a military police guard to stitch the wound of a detainee who was injured after being slammed against a wall in his cell; sodomizing a detainee with a chemical light and perhaps a broom stick, and using military dogs to frighten and intimidate detainees with threats of attack, and in one instance actually biting a detainee.[16]

The report found that in the prison during 2003, there were a series of "sadistic, blatant, and wanton criminal abuses."[17] As a consequence of the incidents, the officer in charge of the prison, army reserve Brigadier General Janis Karpinski was suspended from duties, while seven other suspects faced possible charges under military law.

Perhaps the worst aspect of the case was that the suspects had taken photographs and made videos of the prison guards abusing prisoners. In the report, Taguba states that there were "detailed witness statements and the discovery of extremely graphic photographic evidence." Strangely, it was decided that this evidence was not to be included in Taguba's final reports on the incidents.

The explosive story on the abuse written by Seymour Hersh in the *New Yorker* magazine makes it very clear what these pictures contained.

> The photographs tell it all. In one, Private England, a cigarette dangling from her mouth, is giving a jaunty thumbs-up sign and pointing at the genitals of a young Iraqi, who is naked except for a sandbag over his head, as he masturbates. Three other hooded and naked Iraqi prisoners are shown, hands reflexively crossed over their genitals.[18]

Combined with the details of the abuses, the photos provided powerful evidence of the treatment of Iraqi prisoners. They sent shock waves through the American command structure, which began to slowly realize the damage that could be done to the United States' reputation and, in particular, the U.S. army. Fortunately, at the time of the report, the media were far behind the military on the story and no media organization had received copies of the pictures. This, however, was about to change.

In early 2004, the family of one of the soldiers charged with crimes involving the abuse contacted the website of retired Colonel David Hackworth and informed him that they had copies of the pictures. Colonel Hackworth later contacted CBS and the pictures were passed to the team of *60 Minutes II*. The pictures were now in the hands of the media, but it did not necessarily mean that they would be immediately published!

Using the pictures to explain the abuse, *60 Minutes II* originally proposed to air the story on April 14, 2004, but, before the scheduled broadcast, CBS received a number of calls from the Pentagon that convinced them to hold back the story. The Pentagon was apparently worried that the pictures might inflame tension in Iraq, especially prior to the proposed assault on Falujah where terrorists were intent on making a stand against the U.S. army.[19] Held back for a week, CBS producers decided to air the story on April 21, but once again there were calls from the Pentagon expressing fears that the program would undermine the morale of U.S. troops. There were also concerns about U.S. hostages being held by the terrorists and a worry that the pictures would lead to their execution. This was especially true in the case of American Nick Berg who was being held at the time and the Pentagon believed publication of the pictures would endanger the chances of him being released.[20] To add weight to Pentagon concerns, the Chairman of the Joint Chiefs of Staff General Richard Myers personally phoned Dan Rather, the managing editor of CBS, and asked him not to run the segment. After the phone call, and in discussions with other members of the CBS team, it was agreed that they would once again withhold the story. Held back for two weeks, the program was finally broadcast on April 29, 2004.

When telling the story of how National Guard soldiers were allegedly asked to "prepare" Iraqi prisoners for interrogation by the intelligence services, the *60 Minutes II* story, carried the following candid acknowledgment:

> Two weeks ago, *60 Minutes II* received an appeal from the Defense Department, and eventually from the Chairman of the Joint Chiefs of Staff, Gen. Richard Myers, to delay this broadcast—given the danger and tension on the ground in Iraq. *60 Minutes II* decided to honor that request, while pressing for the Defense Department to add its perspective to the incidents at Abu Ghraib prison. This week, with the photos

beginning to circulate elsewhere, and with other journalists about to publish their versions of the story, the defense department agreed to cooperate in our report.[21]

Based on this statement, it appears that CBS was trying to be both ethical—because it listened to the Pentagon about the dangers—and hard nosed—because it recognized the fact that it was close to being scooped. This was an indirect acknowledgment that Seymour Hersh, who had been sent a copy of Taguba's report, was very close to publishing his own account of the Abu Ghraib scandal. The statement shows, therefore, that when faced with the hard economics of journalism the broadcaster was prepared to jettison Pentagon concerns.

As to what was said between Myers and Rather, the General's appearance before the U.S. Senate Armed Services Committee on May 7, 2004 is extremely illuminating. During the hearing, Senator Mark Dayton D-Minn closely questioned Myers on his attempts to get CBS to hold back the story. To Dayton's question about whom he discussed the CBS issue with, General Myers replied, "This had been worked at lower levels with the [Defense] secretary's staff and my staff for some time."[22] In questioning Myers, Dayton uses the word "suppress" causing General Myers to say, "I called CBS to ask them to delay the pictures showing on CBS's '60 Minutes' because I thought it would result in direct harm."[23]

He later clarified his answer with the following, "This was not to suppress anything. What I asked CBS News to do was to delay the release of the pictures, given the current situation in Iraq, which was as bad as it had been since major combat ended, because I thought it [would] bring direct harm to our troops; it would kill our troops."[24] General Myers also confirmed that the real problem for the Pentagon was the pictorial evidence. When answering Dayton's question about the time period for the intervention with CBS, Myers said, "I did it [the telephone call] based on talking to [the commander of U.S. Central Command] General Abizaid and his worry was like mine, and he convinced me that this was the right thing to do. There was no—this report has been around since January. *What was new were the pictures. I asked for the pictures to be delayed* [emphasis added]."[25] Myers then goes on to refute the claim of suppression leading Dayton to comment:

> I would just say, General—and I agree with your assessment of the consequences of this on our troops, and that's the great tragedy of this, but attempts to suppress news reports, to withhold the truth from Congress and from the American people is antithetical to democracy.... And whatever

the intentions may be, sir, the result is always the same. And it's, I think terribly tragic that the president, who wants to expand democracy around the world, by actions of his own administration is undermining that democracy in the United States.[26]

Dayton's words led Defense Secretary Rumsfeld, who was also attending the hearing before the Senate committee, to defend General Myers's actions:

Throughout the history of this country, there have been instances where military situations have existed that have led government to talk to members of the media and make an editorial request of them that they delay for some period disclosing some piece of information. It is not against our history. It is not against our principles. It is not suppression of the news. And it's a misunderstanding of the situation to say it is.

General Myers's views were later amplified as he toured the television studios to put his case that the military had not sought to censor CBS. On *This Week with George Stephanopolous*, in answer to a question from George Will about the delay, Myers said, "you can't keep this out of the news, clearly, but I thought it was, would be particularly inflammatory at that time."[27] Accepting the fact that the U.S. army was engaged in a bloody fight with the insurgents, it was difficult to believe that General Myers could ever envisage a suitable time to release the pictures!

Elsewhere, on May 2, the General received rather more generous treatment at the hands of the media. Appearing on CBS' *Face the Nation* the General did not have to field questions about Pentagon pressure on the broadcaster. The lack of appetite for the CBS angle was also repeated on the conservative Fox News Channel whose *Fox News Sunday* also failed to ask the General about the scandal. Perhaps it was not unexpected that Fox News would ignore the subject, but CBS' decision to avoid the matter only reinforced the impression that it was involved in damage limitation, as opposed to a genuine attempt to show that the broadcaster had different editorial policies for its programs.

Comments by CBS staff members also gave credence to the idea that, having failed to support the media's independence, damage limitation was probably the best that the broadcaster could hope for. Jeff Fager, executive producer of *60 Minutes II*, said when asked, "News is a delicate thing ... it's hard to just make these kinds of decisions. It's not natural for us, the natural thing is to put it on the air. But the circumstances were quite unusual and I think you have to consider that."[28] The producer also argued that the program was obliged to take safety issues into account,

"There's a war going on and Americans are at risk, especially the ones that are being held hostage. It concerns us."[29]

Indirectly implying that the military intervention may well have helped the quality of the story, Fager also told the AP that, rather than hinder the story, the delay had actually improved it by giving *60 Minutes II* more time to talk to individuals and to seek statements from the military. While this may be so, it is difficult not to see Fager's comments as deeply troubling.

Perhaps it could be argued that there are situations where editors might withhold stories because of the threat to lives—knowledge of the Normandy invasions during World War II might be a good example— but Fager's comments imply that CBS simply divested itself of its editorial responsibility and handed control to the military. If the story needed further investigation then why did program editors fail to insist on this themselves? Moreover, either they were happy with the content to be aired on April 14 or they were not! The abnegation of this editorial responsibility appeared to be a complete breakdown in editorial independence, and the attempt to show that CBS actually profited from it was an exercise in cynical damage control. After all, in a democracy, surely editors have editorial control over their output, not the Chairman of the Joint Chiefs of Staff.

After the release of the pictures, there was widespread criticism of the U.S. military in the international media, particularly from the Arab media. Both Al-Jazeera and Al-Arabiya showed the pictures continuously on their television channels. In Egypt, the newspaper *Akhbar el-Yom* simply called the story a "scandal." Elsewhere, in Kuwait, the influential newspaper *El Watan* stated that the abuses of Iraqi prisoners could heighten tensions in the region and encourage others to join the insurgents.[30]

Within the United States, conservative media launched their own attacks against those media that carried the story, including CBS. On the Fox News Channel, Bill O'Reilly claimed that the publication of the photos was an attempt at undermining an administration fighting a war and that the attacks were motivated by liberal media organizations. Writing on the *National Review Online*, editor-at-large Jonah Goldberg highlighted his own misgivings about CBS' actions.

In an article titled, "Media Missteps," dated May 7, 2004, Goldberg said, "CBS should be ashamed for running the photos."[31] He then went on to question whether the revelation of the pictures was necessary for the actual story: "So the question is, what was gained by releasing these images now? CBS could have reported the story without the pictures. They could have still beaten their competition to the punch."[32] Signing off, Goldberg admitted that the government should not have stopped the publication, but advocated that CBS recognize the danger of publishing the photos. He then invited the broadcaster to censor itself.

Five days after his first article, Goldberg wrote another piece claiming that the cruel death of American Nick Berg was a direct result of the Abu Ghraib photos. Berg was killed in early May and the kidnappers later released a video of his murder on a website that claimed his death resulted from the abuse of the Iraqi prisoners at Abu Ghraib. Although it appeared there might have been a connection, Berg's murder was also similar in nature to that of Daniel Pearl, a journalist from the *Wall Street Journal*, who was killed in Pakistan.

While the media debated the merits of releasing the photos, few commentators took the time to realize that the indirect pressure on CBS closely resembled an earlier event occurring shortly after the September 11 attacks: the Condoleezza Rice telephone call to the heads of the major television broadcasters about the possibility of coded messages in videos made by al Qaeda. Similar to the CBS case, Rice talked about the possibility that the videos could incite Muslim fundamentalists leading to attacks on American citizens.

MEDIA ON THE MARCH (WITH THE BUSH ADMINISTRATION)

National Security Advisor Condoleezza Rice's telephone call to the major broadcasters, including the cable news channels, came in early October 2001. Her decision to do so was prompted by the airing of videotapes sent by al Qaeda calling for attacks on Americans and their property. On October 9, 2001, the broadcasters aired a videotape from al Qaeda spokesperson Suleiman Abu Geith stating that, if the Americans and British failed to leave Afghanistan the "land would burn with fire under their feet, God willing."

On the following day, October 10, 2001, Rice placed a conference call with the media executives of ABC News, CBS News, CNN, Fox News Channel, and NBC. Rice told the executives that security personnel were worried at the inflammatory language of the videotapes and feared that they might contain hidden codes with which to direct other attacks on American soil. She also mentioned that the language could incite Muslims in other countries. While acknowledging the importance of the media, Rice said the executives should give priority to security concerns. At that point, Rice withdrew from the conference call allowing the media executives to discuss the matter on their own.

In their discussion, the media executives agreed that, in future, the videotapes would be heavily edited and greater context would be provided. The executives' decision was unique because it was the first time that the major broadcasters had ever discussed a joint policy on a news issue. Commenting after the discussion, the President of CBS news, Andrew Heyward, said, "This is a new situation, a new war, and a new kind of enemy. Given the historic events we are enmeshed in, it's appropriate to explore new ways of fulfilling our responsibilities to the public."

Because of the situation, Heyward's words were interesting. He implied that the news broadcasters would fulfill their "responsibilities to the public" by heavily editing information that could be in the public interest and newsworthy. As such, the discussion had profound implications for the government's relationship with the media that echoed over four years and found resonance in the case of CBS and the Abu Ghraib pictures. The most worrying aspect was that a media skeptical on almost every other subject found it appropriate to accept the premise of both Rice and General Myers without, first, thinking through the implications for press freedom and editorial independence and, second, reaching a conclusion about whether the assertions were factually correct. Significantly, there have also been other cases where the media have willingly followed an administration's wishes.

One such example was the *New York Times'* scoop that the Kennedy administration was intending to allow the 1961 Bay of Pigs invasion to go ahead. Fearing that the exposure would alert the Cubans to the impending attack and increase the likelihood of large numbers of casualties, editors at the *Times* decided to withhold the story until the attempted invasion had taken place. The decision was evidence that, during a time of crisis, the media were prepared to subordinate their usual watchdog role to national security, and it confirmed Kennedy's own views on the way the media should behave during a time of conflict. Speaking before the American Newspaper Publishers Association on April 27, 1961, just ten days after the attack started, Kennedy said, "Every newspaper asks itself, with respect to every story, 'Is it news?' All I suggest is that you add the question: 'Is it in the national interest of the national security?'"
In the 1980s, ABC discovered evidence of the imminent invasion of Grenada by the U.S. military, but decided to withhold the information out of fear that breaking the story would endanger the lives of American soldiers.

It is arguable that, in these circumstances, the withholding of information is legitimate. There is a clear correlation because the publication of invasion plans could lead to increased casualties. Controversy, however, arises over the actual role that government can play in convincing media organizations to withhold information. In both of the above cases, it would appear that editors wrestled with the dilemma themselves, eventually reaching the conclusion that the reports should be kept back. This compares unfavorably with the pictures in the Abu Ghraib case and the Rice telephone call because the administration took the lead. Whatever the intention of the Bush administration, this initiation of the process creates the undeniable impression that the government is attempting to censor the media.

Interestingly, the *Times'* case had an ending that throws further light on the question and, perhaps, underlines just how important it is for the media to make their own decisions in such matters. After the debacle of the Bay of Pigs that saw the invasion repulsed on Cuba's beaches, President Kennedy told the then publisher of the *Times*, Orvil Dryfoos, that if the newspaper had published the story it might have led to the cancellation of the invasion and saved hundreds of lives. Kennedy's words were further evidence of the need for media organizations to carefully weigh up the newsworthiness of the information based on their own editorial values.

CBS—A BETRAYAL OF NEWS VALUES?

When reviewing the CBS decision to hold back the story of the abuses at the Abu Ghraib prison, it is hard not to see it as a betrayal of news values, and the cherished editorial independence of one of the oldest news broadcasters in the United States. Instead of relying on their own judgment, experienced newsmen including Dan Rather, jettisoned decades of deliberately distancing themselves from sources of power, and accepted the weak assertions of a military General. The decision was not only an affront to the journalism profession; it undermined the convention that the overriding duty of the media is to hold governments to account.

In the Abu Ghraib case, CBS set aside this fundamental principle and happily embraced the weak arguments of a military General, who appeared to be buying time. Would an Iraqi population angered by the sight of the Abu Ghraib pictures lead to increased casualties of American soldiers? What evidence did the General have? Did CBS even ask for evidence?

Regarding the other claim that the pictures would endanger hostages: given the fact that hostages had been killed before, it was unlikely that the release or non-release of the pictures would impact on the decision of the kidnappers. It was claimed that Berg was killed because of the Abu Ghraib pictures, but, as with Daniel Pearl, it was unlikely that he would be released. The decision by the kidnappers to tie Berg's death to the picture release appeared to be more of a deeply cynical afterthought than a strategy. Did CBS ask if the military were involved in ongoing negotiations with the kidnappers? Was there a rescue attempt in the making? Once again, it appears that there was an acceptance of the military's views with no attempt to weigh these arguments against CBS' own need to uphold editorial independence.

In other cases involving the military, it could at least be argued that the danger of increased casualties existed. A catastrophe anyway, the Bay of Pigs may have been worse if Castro had known of the impending attack. American casualties could have been higher in Grenada if the invasion had been publicized beforehand. The difference between these cases and Abu Ghraib was that the media wrestled with the dilemma alone, they weighed up the principles without the military attempting to apply pressure. In the Abu Ghraib case, however, there appeared to be no assessment of the journalistic principles involved, no review of the situation; instead, a major editorial decision was made on the basis of a series of polite, constructive telephone calls with a member of the military.

Why did CBS wait so long before finally broadcasting the *60 Minutes II* program? Reacting to CBS's decision, Bob Steele, The Nelson Poynter Scholar for Journalism at the Poynter Institute for Media Studies, said, "You'd have to be convinced that these other American lives are truly on the line . . . . I would want to have a very specific and short time period [to withhold the news]. If CBS believes [it was] justified [in holding] back two weeks seems like an awful long time. Perhaps a day or two, but two weeks is a long time, particularly with the nature of the allegations on the video."[33]

Steele's comments were direct criticism of the fact that the news broadcaster waited two weeks, and, during that time, postponed the program a second time. If it had not been the threat of the scoop, there is no way of telling how long the broadcaster would have continued to withhold the story!

Significantly, there appears to be a question that the editorial and production staff of *60 Minutes II* failed to ask themselves: In a war is there ever a good time to release news of inhumane behavior perpetrated by the U.S. army? The likely answer is that there is never a good time! If that is true, then the withholding of the story for longer than Steele's "day or two" was the journalistic equivalent of dereliction of duty. It only served to give the military more time to devise a public relations strategy to negate the damage.

This helpful attitude towards the military was also exhibited by broadcasting executives at CBS. Speaking on CNN's *Reliable Sources*, Jim Murphy, a CBS News Executive, said, "You know what? We are like every other American. We want to win this war. We believe in the country."[34] Murphy's words were proof that there was little difference of opinion between editors and executives on the question of the Abu Ghraib pictures. But, once again, Murphy's comments appeared to show no understanding of a media organization's need for editorial independence. Instead, Murphy was expressing a rather typical executive view about the nature of the news; namely, the desire to be all things to all interest groups. In essence, it seems the standing rule of media executives is that where public and government share similar opinions it is best not to cross them.

Murphy's support for the war is another worrying aspect of the CBS story. While it could be expected that individuals in news broadcasting might well support their own country during a war, journalism's ethics would dictate that this view is set aside in order to provide balanced news reporting to their viewers. The comments of the news executive appeared to indicate that CBS was a supporter of the war. The view undermined the broadcaster's independence, making it easier to appreciate why it would hold-off from broadcasting the pictures. After all, the contra of Murphy's words is that the broadcasting of the Abu Ghraib pictures could potentially aid the enemy.

CBS was also guilty of sending mixed signals over its decision to hold off and then suddenly broadcast the pictures. As Christopher Hanson points out in his excellent article in the *Columbia Journalism Review*, CBS got itself into considerable ethical difficulties over the pictures and eventually tied itself in so many knots that anything it said on the subject was extremely unconvincing. In his article titled, "Tortured Logic," the journalist said that by not reporting in a timely fashion out of "concern for human lives" and then reversing this attitude by ignoring the "concern for human lives" to report in a timely fashion, CBS gave the impression that it was self-serving and, if necessary, willing to ignore the principles of journalism.

On reflection, it is difficult to avoid the conclusion that CBS ignored its own ethical obligations to journalism in the face of pressure from the U.S. military. By doing so, it wiped away the memories of other journalists in other periods who fought against attempts by governments to apply pressure. Furthermore, the decision to assist the military was a rejection of decades of editorial independence and, in the long run, will be seen as proof that the media are weaker today than they were two or three decades ago.

Sadly, the CBS case could be another sign that, rather than embracing the notion of watchdog, the media in the United States are rejecting it for another model, that of a commercially driven cheerleader for the foreign policies of America. If this were to happen the principle of impartial and contextualized journalism will have been completely undermined. It would become a practice of the past![35]

Where does the impetus to withhold information from the public stem? With conglomerates squeezing their media holdings ever tighter, there is considerable pressure on news divisions to show a profit. As a consequence, in recent years, media concentration has had an impact on the way media organizations report on the news. The following chapter examines the impact of media concentration, together with another aspect of the modern media world, the ability to increase audience share by slanting news in the direction of the views and beliefs of viewers and readers.

Chapter 6

CONCENTRATING ON BIAS

[Real News is] the news you and I need to keep our freedoms.
— Richard Reeves, Journalist-Historian[1]

DE-RAILING THE NEWS

In January 2001, a train derailment in North Dakota during the early morning became a rallying point for the discussion about media concentration in the United States. On leaving the track, the train spilled a rapidly spreading gas cloud of dangerous anhydrous ammonia fertilizer that threatened the city of Minot, North Dakota. With one person dead, and the cloud liable to suffocate citizens as they slept, the local emergency services sought to contact the local radio station KCJB, the chosen broadcaster for emergency news in the area. Despite several attempts, the emergency services were unable to telephone the station directly and "station employees had to be roused from their homes, causing a big delay."[1]

According to the police, the station was transmitting content sent via a satellite feed and there were no staff present at the station. KCJB is owned by Clear Channel Communications, owner of all six commercial stations in the city and 23 out of the 80 commercial stations across the state of North Dakota. The accusation from the emergency services that people's lives were threatened because of the delay in contacting staff has been denied by Clear Channel Communications. Rebutting the claims, the broadcaster has stated that there was an employee on duty that night but difficulties with the phone line and misunderstandings over the technology caused a breakdown in communications.[2]

Nevertheless, the image of the empty radio station at a time of need became a metaphor for the future of radio stations and other media organizations in the United States. Perhaps unaware that Clear Channel Communications were busy denying the claims, a Democratic senator for North Dakota, Byron L. Dorgan, used the Clear Channel story when discussing media concentration. "Over time, concentration of markets means less competition and we know that less competition is always bad for consumers. . . . The Question is, where does this stop."[3]

The story of the gas cloud raised fears that Clear Channel Communications ownership of all the commercial radio stations in Minot has had a considerable impact. Speaking about the company's influence on news, Ken Crites, a reporter working for the *Minot Daily News*, said, "I get up in the morning and it is a disc jockey reading A.P. [Associated Press] copy. . . . The Canadians could come over the border and we would never know it."[4] The media company has also been known to use part-time disc jockeys and to transfer them from one station to another. According to a *New York Times* article at the time, the use of part-time employees has meant that the six commercial stations in Minot employ only one full-time news person.[5]

Is the story of Minot more apocryphal than truthful? While the image of fully automated commercial radio stations heedless to the pleas of humans was perhaps an overreach, there did appear to be a desire in Clear Channel Communications to centralize news by employing only one staff member across the spectrum of stations. Such a decision reflects the modern approach of some media companies to reduce costs by standardizing the news and minimizing the need for additional staff.

In recent years, there have been increasingly bitter arguments, spurred by the polarization of political debate in the United States, about the impact of media concentration on the news. Many media commentators see the growing concentration in the print and broadcast media as a sign that the plurality of news, and therefore views and opinions, is being lost to an ever-growing belief in commercialization, synergies, and profits. Critics of the media environment say that the loss of voice is actively harming American society and that there is an attendant failure to provide the American people with a variety of different information sources. The result is a glaring lack of awareness about world events, as viewers and readers turn inwards, showing more interest in the lives of celebrities and catastrophes than they do in the decision-making processes of their government.

When weighed against each other, it is obvious that news of celebrities is cheaper in real terms than news of current and foreign affairs. Current and foreign affairs, require expert staff, perhaps bureaus in far away countries, as well as a consideration of context, ethics, and balance. Faced with these difficulties, it seems almost appropriate that media organizations would make the choice to reduce their interest in current affairs. The trouble with such a view is that it reduces news to the bottom line, it forces decisions to be made on a commercial basis without examining the other arguments for maintaining news output that reflects not only the celebrity world, but also the world far away from Hollywood.

Without doubt, in a world where the people of the United States are forced to spend considerable amounts of time earning a living, news can help them maintain a vital link with the outside world. After all, modern democracies require citizens to choose governments and leaders, who, in turn, will make hard decisions about the world in which we live; if there is no information about the actions of government, how can elected officials be judged?

Because of these factors, news is not only information, it is a vital aspect of any democracy. Information informs democracy: allowing decisions to be made and ensuring that there are essential checks and balances on government institutions. A problem, however, arises when the dual nature of news is undermined. In previous times, there has always been a fine line between the two aspects of news: its commercialization within a capitalist society and the essential role it plays within a democracy. Working to maintain these two aspects of news has become increasingly difficult in the modern world as greater pressure is exerted on media organizations to maximize their profits by increasing their share prices. The result has been a flight from hard news into softer, cheaper forms of news.

These trends have also had an influence on reporting in the Iraq War. While it is true that the media in the United States have used large amounts of money to cover the war, the problems that have arisen are not one of coverage; they are one of tone. Criticism of the Bush administration and its involvement in the war does exist on American television, but it is largely marginalized; it exists on the outer fringes of the debate about the war, rather than taking center stage alongside the arguments in support of the war. Tellingly, in the first two years after the invasion of Iraq, this has led to an information vacuum, with support for the war outpacing the critics, creating a false environment and allowing the Bush administration to project its own views almost unhindered.

Such arguments form part of the debate about bias in the media, but they also lay the foundation for another disturbing aspect of media concentration, namely, the desire to create synergies across the borders of huge media conglomerates. The impact of this has already started to be felt, and it will have an increasingly damaging effect on news divisions because, if left unchecked, it will lead to the slow, gradual erosion of the firewalls that have been erected over many years to protect the news from infringements by other divisions. At present, news is already viewed as a commodity that can be mixed and matched with the work of other divisions, such as the book, film, and documentary divisions; but, this flexibility, which obviously maximizes profit, not only dilutes the importance of news, it actively prevents journalists from practicing their profession. All of these competing forces can be seen in the case of Private Jessica Lynch.

SAVING [THE MEDIA FROM] PRIVATE LYNCH

There are few cases involving the media during the Iraq war that provide a better insight into what is happening to the media than the case of Private Jessica Lynch, a 19-year-old supply clerk from Palestine, West Virginia. On March 23, 2003, Lynch's unit was ambushed and Iraqi forces captured her after she became lost in the desert. According to the Pentagon, Lynch had bravely fought her captors and been injured and wounded in the process.

Based on a number of articles on Lynch, officials from the American government were quoted as saying that the young soldier was involved in a fierce exchange of fire with Iraqi troops and that she continued to discharge her weapon until she no longer had any bullets. Almost breathless in its delivery, an article in the *Washington Post* said that Lynch was "fighting to the death. She did not want to be taken alive."[6]

Lynch was later rescued in April 2003. A graphic film released to the media showed American Rangers and Navy Seals entering the hospital in Nasiriyah where Lynch was being held captive. Lynch was subsequently taken to another hospital where she was able to recover from her injuries that included a broken arm, a broken thigh, and a dislocated ankle. After the successful raid, the U.S. spokesperson in Doha said, "Some brave souls put their lives on the line to make this happen, loyal to a creed that they know that they'll never leave a fallen comrade."[7]

Speaking about the raid by American Special Forces, doctors at the hospital said the Iraqi army had left the day before the attack. "We were surprised. Why do this? There was no military, there were no soldiers in the hospital," said, Dr. Anmar Uday.[8]

Naturally, the images of the photogenic Lynch being rescued by heroic special forces was emblematic of the war in Iraq and, as the news story was carried across the world, it provided the allies with a much-needed publicity coup. In a series of linked images, the rescue captured the essence of the Iraq story. The only problem with the account of Lynch's capture and her subsequent rescue was that it had very little to do with reality.

Later investigative reporting showed that Lynch had not been wounded, she had not been tortured, and the raid by the Navy Seals was staged for the cameras. Indeed, her injuries were entirely consistent with a road traffic incident. Dr. Harith al-Houssona, who cared for the injured Lynch, said, "There was no [sign of] of shooting, no bullet inside her body, no stab wound—only road traffic accident. They want to distort the picture. I don't know why they think there is some benefit in saying she has a bullet injury."

Staff at the hospital also offered no resistance to her being returned to the allies, and one doctor had even attempted to send her back to the allied lines in an ambulance. Unfortunately, the allies had fired on the ambulance forcing it to return to the hospital. Later, when reporting on the incident, the BBC's *Correspondent* program found that Lynch's rescue was "one of the most stunning pieces of news management ever conceived."[9]

However, the revelations had still to be uncovered when Lynch's rescue became the primer for an embarrassing fight between the major media companies over the right to tell Lynch's story. During this battle, CBS showed it was prepared to go further than other media organizations in the hope of signing Lynch. In doing so, CBS made representations that undermined the good name of its newsroom and risked a conflict of interest that could have broken down the barrier between news and commerce.

Almost from the start, CBS was determined to beat its nearest competitors for Lynch's signature. In an April 17 letter to the Lynch family from news executive Betsy West, CBS said it could offer "a unique combination of projects that will do justice to Jessica's inspiring story." These included: a prime-time biopic to air on CBS; a news special on MTV (owned, like CBS, by Viacom); a very special episode of MTV's *Total Request Live*; and, a book deal with Simon & Schuster (owned, like CBS and MTV, by Viacom). Two more letters were sent on May 12 from correspondent Jane Clayson, focusing on the possibility of news interviews with the newly liberated soldier.

Central to the CBS proposal was a film about Lynch. In a letter to the Lynch family, West said, "CBS Entertainment 'tell us this would be the highest priority for the CBS movie division.' "[10] Fast on the heels of CBS was NBC that, while seeking the rights to the story, had also communicated a desire to continue with the project even if it failed in the attempt.[11]

Criticism of CBS centered on the company's pursuit of a commercial deal while also seeking to interview Lynch for its news division. In an editorial on the subject, the *Charleston Gazette* said, "The need for journalistic independence should be self-evident. Reporters have a hard enough time trying to get to the truth without having to worry about spoiling a book deal or insulting Jah Rule (who was rumored to be willing to sing at a special concert to be attended by Lynch) and blowing the MTV Special."[12] The editorial went on to say, "A half-century ago, when television was new and the great Edward R. Murrow was in his prime, CBS set an example for the rest of broadcast journalism. The fear is that CBS still is setting an example."[13] Other newspapers joined in the criticism of CBS, particularly the *New York Times*, which had broken the original story.

In the face of criticism, CBS was bullish in its defense. Alluding to the Jayson Blair scandal at the *New York Times*, a CBS statement said, "Unlike the *New York Times'* own ethical problems, there is no question about the accuracy or integrity of CBS News' reporting."[14]

However, CBS later appeared to reconsider whether it had broken the traditional firewall between news and entertainment. CBS Chairman, Leslie Moonves, said that the broadcaster should have acted differently. "Maybe...[the biopic] went over the line. That was not respecting, possibly, the sanctity of CBS news.... Probably, if we had to do it all over again, a movie of the week never would have been mentioned in the letter."

Despite their willingness to highlight the problems of news staff at CBS, other news organizations failed to identify what was perhaps the main worry about commercial deals inside media organizations that also happen to be chasing news: the distinct possibility that both sides of the firewall may find themselves in a conflict of interest. Using the Lynch situation as an example, what would have happened in the news division of CBS if they had discovered that certain aspects of the Lynch story were untrue? Would they face pressure from other divisions of the media organization to keep quiet about these discoveries out of fear of jeopardizing the other media projects? These questions highlight the problem where those who are the focus of news are also seen as possible revenue earners for the company.

Of course, this did not happen in the Lynch case; another media organization, the BBC, broke the story that the Pentagon had been economical with the truth about Lynch's injuries and her rescue. Given the commercialization and over-concentration in the American media market, however, the hypothetical situation outlines the dangers faced by journalists. It represents a world where hard news and the work of journalists are subordinated to allow book and film divisions to reap the rewards of commercial deals.

The desire to make money from certain newsworthy individuals is one of the underlying problems of media concentration. With executives ever eager to make profits from their news divisions, no one appears to have considered the dangers of seeing news events as possible entertainment. The effect will be to dilute the importance of news and to risk the possibility of downgrading factual events to such an extent that they become yet another feature of the entertainment world.

If this were to happen, the firewalls will be torn away and the following will occur: news will be stripped of its credibility and the audience will have no ability to differentiate between the values of news and other forms of entertainment. In turn, unable to differentiate fact from mere assertion or entertainment, the audience will revert to their own assumptions about the world, differentiating facts according to their own bias as opposed to their belief in the veracity of news. Attendant to this problem is a rise in public apathy. In effect, the problem is in danger of becoming a self-fulfilling prophecy with the public turning off because of the loss of veracity, forcing media organizations to do more to make the news more entertainment-orientated and, according to the prevailing belief, more interesting.

In effect, these trends in the media sound the death knell for unbiased, factual reporting. It reveals a news world where events and facts have been loosened from their moorings and allowed to float in a sea clouded by conjecture, opinion, and bias.

Sadly, the pressures on news from within the media industry have arisen at the same time that, in the political sphere, facts are becoming dangerously politicized. The war in Iraq was posited on the assertion that there were WMD and that Saddam Hussein represented a realizable threat to the United States. The quick destruction of Saddam's forces, weakened by years of an arms embargo, and the failure of the allied forces to find WMD, seriously damaged the allied intelligence services, and led to the accusation from those who disagreed with the war that the intelligence information had been corrupted to support the drive for war.

The result is a nagging fear among the public that the institutions tasked with providing them with solid factual information are failing them. Despite warnings about shooting the messenger, the media, which did little to test the evidence of the Bush administration, have been tarred with the same brush.

There are connections between the two institutions of politics and the media. On March 6, 2003, during a press conference for the U.S. media, President Bush evoked al Qaeda and the September 11 attacks 14 times.[15] The assembled journalists failed to question the president on this issue and ask him why he believed in a connection between September 11 and Iraq for which there is simply no evidence. Unforgivably, the mainstream media lent credence to this view by communicating the president's words without questioning their validity.

Speaking at the Schumann Center for Media and Democracy in November 2003, Bill Moyers gave the following warning,

> media giants . . . exalt commercial values at the expense of democratic value. . . . In so doing they are squeezing out the journalism that tries to get as close as possible to the verifiable truth; they are isolating serious coverage of public affairs into ever-dwindling "news holes" or far from prime- time; and they are gobbling up small and independent publications competing for the attention of the American people.

In a globalized world that is supposed to bring everyone closer together as well as improve our understanding of the world, it is ironic that trends in news and politics have forced individuals back to responding to the world around them based on their own visceral beliefs as opposed to hard facts. News now risks being drawn into the deep pit of entertainment, and if this were to happen, it is unlikely that it would be able to claw itself out again.

Adding to these problems are the dangers of news being communicated through the prism of bias. As with the commercialization of news, this is not necessarily a style choice, but a sound business practice based on an understanding of demographics and polls.

BIAS: A MATTER OF PERSPECTIVE

In an editorial, revered journalist Walter Cronkite made an admission that might have surprised his many admirers. He said: "I believe that most of us reporters are liberal, but not because we consciously have chosen that particular color in the political spectrum. . . . The perceived liberalism of television reporters is a product of limited time given for any particular item. The reporter desperately tries to get all the important facts and essential viewpoints, but, against a fast approaching deadline, he or she must summarize in a sentence the complicated story."[16]

Cronkite was expressing the view that he felt journalists drifted into liberalism because of the nature of the medium and not because of their own political beliefs. The declaration was a deliberate attempt to move away from previous comments by other noteworthy commentators that, in outlook and background, journalists are liberal by nature. Although difficult to prove, Cronkite's words are evidence that the mainstream media is extremely sensitive about accusations of bias and, on occasion, it has done its utmost to deflect these criticisms. The media's concerns about displays of bias, from either left or right, are also reflected in the way the public views journalism.

Inevitably, the perception of bias is also closely connected to a news organization's credibility. Fears about this have existed for a long time, but an analysis of the problems did not really start until fairly recently. In 1985, a report conducted on behalf of the American Society of Newspaper Editors (ASNE) found that 75 percent of those polled believed that the media had problems with credibility. In an August 2002 poll, the Pew Research Center for the People and the Press found that the percentage of respondents who rated their daily newspaper highly believable had fallen from 80 to 59 percent.

Regarding actual perceptions of bias, in 1986 Robert Lichter, Linda Lichter, and Stanley Rothman released *The Media Elite: America's New Power Brokers*, which reviewed the findings of a 1980 survey of 238 journalists drawn from leading media. On the subject of political views, the survey found that 54 percent of the journalists viewed themselves as being left-of-center, 29 percent as occupants of the middle ground, and 17 percent as being right of center. According to the results of the survey there was a ratio of 3 liberal journalists for every conservative one.[17] The findings appeared to be supported by a 1985 survey in the *Los Angeles Times* that found 55 percent of the journalists sampled to be liberal and 17 percent, conservative.[18]

More recently, a Pew Research Center for the People and the Press survey in 2004 found that, with regard to journalists drawn from national outlets, 34 percent saw themselves as liberal compared to 7 percent who were conservative. Comparing the study to one undertaken in 1995, the Center found that, in terms of respondents who were national journalists, 34 percent of the 2004 sample were liberals, an increase of 12 percent from 1995. Without doubt, journalists as a profession see themselves as more liberal in outlook than conservative; however, the question remains whether this is actually translated into a bias reflected in the newspapers, radio and television stations of the United States.

One of the problems with the "Liberal journalists + News = Liberal Views Expressed as News" equation is that media organizations, as commercial profit centers, are innately conservative in their outlook and views. The fact that, with few exceptions, media organizations have shareholders, accentuates the overall conservatism of these organizations. The idea that liberalism of journalists creates outlaw news divisions, acting unchecked to express the liberal views is simply untrue. Newsrooms have always fought for their independence against the pressures of the business and advertising, but, in today's media environment, as the private Lynch case reveals they are beginning to lose out. The reality is that journalists are fighting for their independence, but not necessarily the right to express liberal values.

Moreover, as the Cronkite statement mentions, journalists are perhaps their own worst enemies. Constantly criticized, many journalists appear to have bought the idea that they express their views through their work As such, the argument that liberal journalists are biased is being used as the siege machine that is slowly breaking down the doors of the American media's independence.

Instead of berating themselves for their perceived liberalism, journalists should ask themselves how it is possible that jury members in American court rooms can, with the full support of the judicial system, convincingly put aside their own bias and reach decisions in the criminal courts, whereas the typical left-wing journalist supposedly floods every story with his or her own bias? Surely, if the American juror can be trusted to make decisions dispassionately, the same can be said for the average journalist.

Unfortunately, if you examine the prevailing view in American, the answer to this question appears to be an overwhelming "no!" According to many, journalists cannot be trusted to exclude bias from their writing, no matter how many practice codes they adhere to. For this reason, American journalists face a tirade of criticism that has its origins in the government, the public, talk show hosts, and pressure groups. The result is a truism, accepted by almost everyone: journalists are biased.

News is also being assaulted from the conservative side. Accepting the news is liberal principle, other media in recent decades have fought back and embraced the conservative perspective in the desire to counterbalance alleged imbalances. Perhaps the most successful example of this trend is the Fox News Channel ("Fox News"). Fox News is the brainchild of Rupert Murdoch who saw within the United States' congested media market an opportunity to represent a missing group within the country: the voiceless conservatives of middle America.

Commenting on the perceived bias of Fox News, the then Chairman of the Board, Roger Ailes, said, "We just broadened the dialogue and broadened the debate. That allowed us to get a foothold because nobody had ever seen that before. The only conservative to ever do television prior to [Fox News] was [columnist] Bob Novak. So there were four hundred liberals and Bob Novak. The public knew that."[19]

Funded by media owner Rupert Murdoch, the positioning of Fox News was brilliantly undertaken by Ailes who had considerable experience in the television business. Originally starting out in commercial television and then working with presidential candidates, Ailes had an almost preternatural appreciation of what the public wanted. Forced to work on a fairly tight budget, Ailes took the formulas of the terrestrial broadcasters, reworked them, and gave the programming a conservative spin. American audiences had never seen television packaged in this manner before and, within a relatively short space of time, the channel had healthy viewing figures.

With a Republican president installed in the White House and a new mood in the country, one widely seen as a rejection of President Clinton's own administration, Fox News was always likely to strike a chord with some parts of the country. However, the events of September 11, 2001, and the subsequent wars in Afghanistan and Iraq, together with the new mood of patriotism, lifted the cable channel from a mere competitor to both Cable News Network (CNN) and the terrestrial channels into one of the most popular television channels in the United States. As a result, irrespective of political or social beliefs, it should be recognized that Murdoch's decision to spend enormous amounts of money on creating a rival to CNN was one of the most intelligent decisions in the history of American television.

Overtaking CNN's *Larry King Live* as the most popular show on cable television, the *O'Reilly Factor* is a good example of the way in which Fox News presents information. A journalist, emmy winner, and holder of a Master's in Public Administration from the Kennedy School of Government, Bill O'Reilly originally presented a syndicated show called *Inside Edition* before moving to Fox News to anchor the *O'Reilly Factor*. The show is devoted to a mixture of O'Reilly's views on current news events, feedback from viewers, and a final interview. It is the last segment of the show that has made O'Reilly notorious and it is one of the reasons for the show's high ratings.

O'Reilly has a strong reputation for his confrontational interviewing style, and while it may lead some viewers to switch off, his show is popular among millions of viewers for the off-hand manner he treats some guests and for the directness of his questioning. Typically, his victims tend to be liberals, who O'Reilly does his best to savage. His approach has led to some heated encounters, with the journalist dismissing his guest if they annoy or irritate him. On one occasion, according to the book *Crazy Like a Fox*, O'Reilly's approach led actress Susan Sarandon, who had been discussing aggressive policing in New York, to ask the journalist's producer, "What's the matter with him?"[20]

Despite his denials, O'Reilly does approach his show from a conservative perspective. The show fits neatly into the cable channel's overall theme of reporting news in a way that is satisfactory to conservative middle America. Moreover, while O'Reilly claims that he has been known to criticize the Bush administration, his views are largely informed by conservative criticism of the president.[21]

Another of O'Reilly favorite phrases is "Shut-up" which he has used against guests who annoy him. Rather than obscuring his arguments and upsetting his audience, O'Reilly's use of pejoratives is seen as reflecting the viewer's own beliefs. In this way, O'Reilly's popularity stems from his ability to identify with his audience and he has gone to considerable lengths to project this image. O'Reilly has made frequent barbs against the French ever since their refusal to agree to a final resolution at the United Nations Security Council, prior to the Iraq war. In the wake of the failed resolution, O'Reilly encouraged his viewers to boycott French goods and he has strongly criticized the actions of President Chirac.

Like O'Reilly, Fox News has consistently denied its conservative bias. Addressing the subject in an article in the *New York Daily News*, Ailes has said, "We're not programming to conservatives. We're just not eliminating their point of view."[22] Though he denied bias in the media organization he headed, Ailes, who is a long time Republican supporter, has also been accused of bias that detractors say is reflected in Fox News. In 2002, Ailes admitted that the story contained in Bob Woodward's *Bush at War* was true and that shortly after the September 11 attacks he had written to President Bush encouraging him to use "the harshest measures possible" to retain the support of the American public. Rebutting the suggestion of bias, Ailes said he wrote to the president as a human being and as a citizen.

On the question of biased news programming, the former producer of news at Fox News, Charlie Reina, has provided a detailed insight into how the cable channel works. Writing to Jim Romenesko at the Poynter Institute, Reina said,

> The roots of [Fox News Channel's] day-to-day on-air bias are actual and direct. They come in the form of an executive memo distributed electronically each morning, addressing what stories will be covered and, often, suggesting how they should be covered. To the newsroom personnel responsible for the channel's daytime programming, The Memo is the bible. If, on any given day, you notice that the Fox anchors seem to be trying to drive a particular point home, you can bet The Memo is behind it.[23]

As an example, Reina provides an account of the cable channel's bias in an executive memo dated March 20, "There is something utterly incomprehensible about Kofi Annan's remarks in which he allows that his thoughts are 'with the Iraqi people.' One could ask where those thoughts were during the 23 years Saddam Hussein was brutalizing those same Iraqis. Food for thought.' " Commenting on this, Reina says, "Can there be any doubt that The Memo was offering not only 'food for thought,' but a direction for the [Fox News Channel] writers and anchors to go? Especially after describing the U.N. Secretary General's remarks as 'utterly incomprehensible?' "[24]

On the vexed question of suicide bombers, Reina said that Fox management distributed a memo discussing whether the cable channel should describe the attacks as "homicide bombings," a line of thought that appeared to follow the Bush administration's thinking on the subject. In his e-mail, Reina said, "These are not isolated incidents at Fox News Channel, where virtually no one of authority in the newsroom makes a move unmeasured against management's politics, actual or perceived. At the Fair and Balanced network, everyone knows management's point of view, and in case they're not sure how to get it on air, The Memo is there to remind them."[25]

Further evidence of the cable channel's bias came with a year-long study at the University of Maryland that reported Americans who relied on Fox News had serious misperceptions regarding the war in Iraq. According to the study, when asked questions concerning al Qaeda's support for Iraq, Saddam's Hussein's involvement in the September 11 attacks and the belief that WMD had been found, higher percentages of Fox News viewers believed in the truth of these statements when compared to the viewers of other broadcasters. In an article about the study, the *Washington Post* reported, "The fair and balanced folks at Fox, the survey concludes, were 'the news source whose viewers had the most misperceptions.' Eighty percent of Fox viewers believed at least one of these un-facts; 45 percent believed all three."[26]

An article in the *Wall Street Journal* in 2005 also damaged the credibility of the news organization. Writing on the subject of the BBC's license fee in the United Kingdom, Scott Norvell, the London chief of Fox News, wrote, "Even we at Fox News manage to get some lefties on the air occasionally, and often let them finish their sentences before we club them to death and feed the scraps to Karl Rove and Bill O'Reilly. And those who hate us can take solace in the fact that they aren't subsidizing Bill's bombast; we payers of the BBC license fee don't enjoy that peace of mind."[27]

Norvell went on to say, "Fox News is, after all, a private channel and our presenters are quite open about where they stand on particular stories. That's our appeal. People watch us because they know what they are getting. The Beeb's institutionalized leftism would be easier to tolerate if the corporation was a little more honest about it."[28]

While free expression and the need for a plurality of views means that the Fox News channel has a perfect right to broadcast information in the way it does, its strident position is particularly damaging not only to journalism, but also for the public. The fact that its viewers have mis-perceptions about the war in Iraq leads to the undeniable conclusion that news in America is being undermined by a vicious struggle between right and left; significantly, the political vortex created by this struggle has sucked in all of the media. At peril in this fight are news and facts that are increasingly being seen as propaganda for those who would advocate a political position.

WHO'S SORRY NOW!

The pressure on news in the United States clearly affected the reporting of the Iraq war. With opinion polls in the media revealing that the public accepted various distortions regarding the September 11 attacks, it was inevitable that the public would make a strong connection between these misperceptions and the war in Iraq.

In effect, the misperceptions helped maintain support for the decision to invade Iraq and it allowed the Bush administration to put its war plans into action without fear of public support evaporating. Unfortunately, the buoyant support for the war was gained at a cost for news and the news values that go with it.

These pressures on news reporting are not new; they are merely part of the ongoing battle, fought over decades, that has seen facts, as opposed to their interpretation, continually questioned as part of the vicious political fight between right and left. The problem is that while this might have short-term gains for those seeking support for their views, the long-term loss of politicizing news is applicable to everyone in equal measure.

In recent years, and most notably in the lead-up to the war in Iraq, factual reporting has been dragged from the center and been violently pulled at from both sides of the political spectrum. Under assault for decades because of their perceived liberalism, many journalists have also retreated from seeking to inform to the standby position of merely laying out information for public consumption. In some cases, this can be a worthy exercise, but it fails completely when facts need to be questioned or interpreted. Along with the movement towards greater media concentration, which has sought to force news to collude with entertainment, these trends have so radicalized factual reporting that in the Iraq war, obvious falsehoods have come to be accepted, while, on occasion, the truth has been rejected.

Due to the assault on the value awarded to facts, the public's ability to make informed decisions has been seriously degraded. In the past, it was possible to agree on the facts, allowing the interpretation of those facts to be argued over. However, during the war in Iraq, it was impossible to follow this trusted formula; moreover, with the growing distrust of journalism fuelled by political agendas, the public was forced back into the arms of a government that had strong reasons for distorting the need to go to war.

Played with consummate skill by the Bush administration, the process was surprisingly simple. First, politicize facts to such an extent that journalism can be seen as partisan. Second, drive the public back to accepting the statements of politicians at face value, thus removing the need for the public to make assessments based on the interpretations and evaluations of the media. Such a process is the dream of politicians because it allows for the public's direct consumption of their words (and facts) without the interference of journalism.

The problem for all the parties—the public, the media, and the politicians—is the cost of victory. In denigrating journalists and encouraging the rise of partisan media, politicians are creating a media landscape that will eventually undermine their own work. Separated from the media, which traditionally plays the role of information provider, the public has increasingly relied on politicians to assess the need for war in Iraq. After the failure to find WMD, these so-called facts were later found to be highly dubious and it is unlikely that, in the future, the public will be so trusting of government.

The result is that in seeking to go to war in Iraq, the executive branch has not only degraded journalism, it has also degraded itself. At present, in the United States, facts have become so highly politicized that there is a danger they will never return to the center ground, which would once again allow individuals and groups to agree on the facts, but argue over interpretation.

Interestingly, out of the two institutions—journalism and the executive—it has been journalism that has realized the dangers of this move. The months and years following the Iraq war have seen some media organizations evaluating the way in which they reported on the war in Iraq and appraising whether there is a need for a change of approach. One such media organization was the *New York Times* that led the way in the painful, and potentially harmful, re-examination of way the war was reported.

Chapter 7

MEA PULPA

Once I stepped into the past, I reasoned, I might never find my
way back to the present.
—Daniel Okrent, Public Editor, The *New York Times*,
May 30, 2004

We have studied the allegations of official gullibility and hype.
It is past time we turned the same light on ourselves.
—From the Editors, The *New York Times*, 26 May, 2005

SHINING THE LIGHT

In Michael R. Gordon's and Judith Miller's September 8, 2002, article
titled, "U.S. Says Hussein Intensifies Quest for A-Bomb Parts," the two
journalists claimed that aluminum tubes, intercepted on their way to Iraq,
were to be used as centrifuges in the process of making an atomic bomb.[1]
The article said Iraqi defectors had told American officials that nuclear
arms were once again a top priority and that Hussein had praised his top
Iraqi officials for "their efforts as part of his campaign against the West."[2]
The article also included the following quote:

> Hard-liners are alarmed that American intelligence underestimated the
> pace and scale of Iraq's nuclear program before Baghdad's defeat in the
> [first] gulf war. Conscious of this lapse in the past, they argue that
> Washington dare not wait until analysts have found hard evidence that
> Mr. Hussein has acquired a nuclear weapon. The first sign of a 'smoking
> gun,' they argue, may be a mushroom cloud.[3]

Administration officials were quick to use the article from the liberal
leaning newspaper as proof of the situation's seriousness. Using the

powerful imagery of the "mushroom cloud," members of the Bush administration mentioned the *New York Times* article when they appeared on Sunday morning television talk shows. The article became proof of the need for action against Hussein, and it did much to dampen opposition to the war in America. The opponents of war had argued against the invasion of Iraq, but found it difficult to do so when the country's most influential newspaper also appeared to be arguing the case for war.

Contrary to the strident language, essential elements of Gordon's and Miller's September 8 story were either incorrect or false. The story was long on gullibility and short on a journalist's essential tool: healthy skepticism in the face of claims made by those who may well have an interest in the outcome of the story. For example, the much discussed aluminum tubes were apparently covered with a coating that needed to be removed before the tubes could be successfully used as centrifuges; however, the removal process would have interfered with the thickness of the tubes, making them useless for their apparent purpose. Nuclear scientists also disputed claims that the tubes were part of Iraq's nuclear weapons program; the scientists pointed out that the nuclear weapons industry had long ago replaced aluminum tubes with steel ones. Other scientists said it was likely the tubes were to be used in a multiple launch rocket system; a theory supported by the name stamped on the tubes, "Medusa 81," the model of a rocket built in Italy.[4]

Commentators have pointed to the source of the story as Adnan Ihsan Saeed, a defector who was apparently brought to Miller's attention by Ahmad Chalabi, one of the leading Iraqi defectors and a friend of hawks both in and around the Bush administration. During conversations with Miller, Saeed apparently told the *New York Times* journalist that he had been employed in Hussein's nuclear weapons program and that the dictator had a series of weapons establishments currently being repaired in order to restart the program. As James C. Moore points out in his article, "Not Fit to Print" in *Salon* such establishments turned out to be non-existent.[5]

Another article by Miller titled, "Illicit Arms Kept Till Eve of War, Iraqi Scientist Is Said to Assert," and published by the *New York Times* on April 21, 2003, carried the assertions of an Iraqi scientist that the journalist had never actually interviewed.[6] The article told readers about a man in the desert pointing to an area that he said contained the precursors needed for WMD—a man described to Miller by her contacts within the Mobile Exploration Team Alpha of the U.S. Army.

Once again, Miller's story was used by supporters of the Bush administration to justify the invasion of Iraq. Moreover, the article was used by local newspapers in the United States who changed the headline to make the article even more suggestive. "Illegal Material Spotted" said the *Rocky Mountain News*, while the *Seattle Post-Intelligencer* said, "Outlawed Material Destroyed by the Iraqis Before the War."[7] Such stories further impressed upon the American public the notion that WMD existed and, coming from the *New York Times*, the paper of record, they provided a justification for the Bush administration's actions.

Not everyone was happy with these news reports and, in the aftermath of the Iraq war, there was growing disquiet at the way in which the media had reported. The failure of the Iraqi survey group to find WMD only served to amplify this criticism. Because of its importance within the American media environment much of this criticism was aimed at the *New York Times* and Miller's reporting. No doubt aware of the criticism and perhaps stung by it, the newspaper made an attempt in the early part of 2004 to set the record straight.

HOLD THE FRONT (OR PERHAPS THE MIDDLE) PAGE

In an article written on March 30, Rick Mercier of the *Free Lance-Star* wrote that much of the media should be apologizing for its reporting on Iraq. Acknowledging that the media was beginning to question the quality of intelligence analyzing the Iraq threat in the lead-up to the war, Mercier commented:

> Most of these media outlets, however, also need to conduct self-examinations. From the horrendously distorted coverage of *Times* reporter Judith Miller (her sins in many ways were far worse than those of plagiarist/fabricator Jayson Blair) to the bewildering (and biased?) news judgment of the *Posts*' editors, journalists at America's most influential publications helped ensure that a majority of you would be misinformed about Iraq and the nature of the threat it posed to you.[8]

Mercier's article appeared to have the desired impact on the mainstream media. On May 26, 2004, the *New York Times* shone the light of investigation upon itself. In an article of 1,174 words, the newspaper tried to reconcile some of its reporting in the lead-up to the war with what had or had not been discovered by the Iraqi Survey Group. According to the newspaper:

> In most cases, what we reported was an accurate reflection of the state of our knowledge at the time, much of it painstakingly extracted from

intelligence agencies that were themselves dependent on sketchy information. And where those articles included incomplete information or pointed in a wrong direction, they were later overtaken by more and stronger information. That is how news coverage normally unfolds.[9]

Despite these assurances, the *New York Times*' statement from the editors went on to say, "We found a number of instances of coverage that was not as rigorous as it should have been. In some cases, information that was controversial then, and seems questionable now, was insufficiently qualified or allowed to stand unchallenged." The newspaper then offered the following, "Looking back, we wish we had been more aggressive in re-examining the new claims as new evidence emerged—or failed to emerge."[10]

The *Times* then returned to a number of articles published both before and after the war in Iraq. Much of the self-criticism was directed at the newspaper's failure to follow-up on stories it reported. This failure gave readers the impression that the *Times* stood by the original story; however, the newspaper failed to inform its readers that the accounts had not been "independently verified," and that information provided by informants had not been proven by later events. For example, the *Times*' statement referred to stories dated October 26 and November 1, 2001, describing secret Iraqi camps where "Islamic terrorists were trained and chemical and biological weapons used."[11] The *Times*' statement commented that such stories had never been verified by sources that were independent. Quoting Michael Gordon in *The New York Review of Books*, the editors' note states, "We consider the story of Iraq's weapons, and of the pattern of misinformation, to be unfinished business. And we fully intend to continue aggressive reporting aimed at setting the record straight."[12]

The words contained in the statement were bravely said and they revealed an institution that was at least prepared to go through a painful period of self-examination regarding its own involvement in the misinformation that was delivered to the public. Despite this, however, much of the discussion after the release of the statement centered around the question whether the newspaper had gone far enough in the review of its reporting.

One of the problems with the editors' note was its desire to tie the *Times*' own reporting to what was known by the government—"in this case it looks as if we, along with the administration, were taken in. And, until now we have not reported that to our readers." The newspaper also wanted to keep the door open to the possibility that, "it is still possible that chemical or biological weapons will be unearthed in Iraq." Such statements appeared self-serving; especially when they were delivered in what should have been an objective self-examination.

The *Times* was also wrong to allow itself to be hoodwinked; particularly when it appeared to dismiss out of hand the possibility that it was the Bush administration who had been doing the hoodwinking. The *Times'* refusal to acknowledge the complicated "echo chamber" it was working in, also appears to be naïve. At no time does the *Times* acknowledge the possibility that it had been used not only to promote public support for the war, but also as proof that the reasons for war were capable of being independently verified by a highly respected newspaper.

Concerns about the *Times* note also arose within the newspaper itself. Writing four days after the publication of the editors' note, the *Times'* Public Editor, Daniel Okrent, "mostly" praised the decision, but agreed with a reader who had asked whether Okrent would comment on why the editors' note had appeared on A10 and not been mentioned on the front page.[13]

Responding to the editors' note, Okrent said, "The *Times'* flawed journalism continued in the weeks after the war began, when writers might have broken free from the cloaked government sources who had insinuated themselves and their agendas into the prewar coverage."[14] Okrent then outlined several areas where he felt the newspaper could improve its reporting— these areas included a reordering of priorities, such as downscaling the desire to be first, and a timely reflection on the use of government sources. The article by Okrent represents possibly the best examination of the editors' note and the fact that it was published in the *Times'* lent greater credibility to what the newspaper was trying to achieve with its critical re-evaluation.

Other commentators also provided their views. David Rubin, Dean of the Newhouse School of Public Communications at Syracuse University, was quoted as saying that the editors' note was necessary because the newspaper had found itself "in a perfect storm" of the interests of Iraqi exiles and those of the Bush administration. "It was formed by the congruence of a group of Iraqis who wanted regime change and the Bush administration that wanted regime change," Rubin said.[15]

On NPR's *Talk of the Nation*, Robert Steele, the Nelson Poynter Scholar for Journalism Values at the Poynter Institute, said, by acting in this way, the "*New York Times* is acknowledging that they didn't do as good a job as they should have in bringing some level of balance in there in terms of the allegations, in terms of the assumptions, in terms of what the wind blowing messages were."[16] Asked by the program's host, Neal Conan, about the appropriate relationship between government and the media, Steele replied, "[O]ne of the lynchpin principles of journalism is independence, an obligation to be very vigorous and rigorous in holding the powerful accountable, including government officials. And we also must make sure that we're not unduly influenced by those who have position or power."[17]

In general, there appeared to be an acceptance that the editors' note, although belated, was a genuine attempt at setting the record straight. Some, however, questioned the failure of the *Times'* to name Judith Miller as the journalist who was involved in writing many of the offending articles. A consistent critic of Miller, *Slate* magazine writer Jack Shafer caustically wrote in his article, "The *Times* Scoop That Melted," "If reporters who live by their sources were obliged to die by their sources, *New York Times* reporter Judith Miller would be stinking up her family tomb right now." The article then went on to list some of the journalist's apparently faulty journalism.[18]

In 2005, Shafer called for an exorcism to be carried out at the *Times*. The journalist argued that the *Times* should only be allowed to escape the question of its reporting on WMD once it had carried out a thorough review of its reporting, similar to that undertaken when Jayson Blair was exposed for false news reporting [19] "What the paper never did— even in its mini culpa—was to account for how [Miller] . . . consistently snaked her bogus stories into the *Times* before and after the invasion. The mini culpa never mentions Miller or any other reporters by name, the implication being that the failure wasn't just individual but institutional, a notion I support."[20]

Miller has been defended by the *Times'* executive editor Bill Keller who refused to name and shame individual journalists. Keller told reporters that the editors' note was "not an attempt to find a scapegoat or to blame reporters for not knowing then what we know now . . . (it) will not satisfy our most vociferous critics, but it is not written for them. It is an attempt to set the record straight, something we do as a point of journalistic pride."[21]

Ironically, another of Miller's defenders is the former *Times'* executive editor, Howell Raines, who said that neither the work of Miller nor that of the editors who supervised her work was rushed or reckless. On the question of placing rough or incomplete articles in the newspaper, Raines said that the front-page meetings held prior to the Iraq war were evidence of the story's seriousness. While both men are protective of Miller they differ on other aspects of the overall story. Keller has consistently sought to highlight the defects at the time, whereas Raines refused to accept that it was the procedures in place that were at fault.

With present and former executive editors disagreeing over the decision, Martin Kaplan, of the Norman Lear Center, provided one of the best comments about the note, "[F]or people who are serious and thoughtful, the *Times* is a gatekeeper of quality in terms of what's credible and believable. When it published those pieces, it sent signals which legitimized our going to war and calmed people's fears that we were rushing. It turns out that the *Times* was hoodwinked just like the rest of the country."[22]

Kaplan's statement put into perspective the differing views of those who vacillated between wanting to see Judith Miller dismissed from the *New York Times* and those who, like Keller, believed that the institution had caused the problem. Seen from these widely different vantage points, the editors' note was never going to please everyone, but it did what the *Times* is respected for: it led the way on one of the most difficult and complicated issues that American newspapers have ever had to deal with. The *New York Times'* house may not have been in order, but it recognized that it had cleaning to do! Moreover, the editors' note encouraged other media organizations also to come forward.

FOLLOW THE "LEADER"

Traditionally within the American media scene, the *New York Times* leads the way on important news subjects. Because of its reputation, the newspaper has a considerable hold on the minds of other journalists, other media organizations; this is particularly true of broadcasters and it can cause journalists to hold back on stories until the *Times* has reported it. In a strange irony, the brave, albeit late, decision of Keller to face the newspaper's critics encouraged other media to apologize. Although this may be seen as evidence of the media's herd mentality, it also represented a growing belief among journalists that the media were accountable to their audience.

Not wishing to be left out, in August 2004, the *Times'* biggest competitor on stories of national import, the *Washington Post*, published its own mea culpa. Speaking of the *Post's* own reporting on WMD, Executive Editor, Leonard Downie Jr. commented, "[W]e were so focused on trying to figure out what the administration was doing that we were not giving the same play to people who said it wouldn't be a good idea to go to war and were questioning the administration's rationale."[23] *The Post* admitted that the statements of the Bush administration often appeared on the front page while anything that might contradict their views appeared "on A18 on Sunday or A24 on Monday."[24]

One of the *Post*'s star reporters and an Assistant Managing Editor, Bob Woodward, went further in his own estimation of the reporting carried out during this period. One of the best-sourced political journalists in Washington, Woodward, through two books on the Bush administration, has provided an incomparable insight into the way the administration works and the tensions that arose over the war in Iraq.[25] "We did our job, but we didn't do enough, and I blame myself mightily for not pushing harder." Woodward then went on to admit that the *Post* failed to tell its readers that the justification for war was "shakier" than believed at the time and that the information they did have should have been front-page news.[26]

In "The *Post* on WMDs: An Inside Story" media reporter Howard Kurtz provided a detailed review of the reporting in that period.[27] Unlike the *Times*, however, Kurtz's story appeared on page 1. Using Woodward's expression, Kurtz admits that journalists at the *Post* were involved in "groupthink" on the subject of WMD, meaning that everyone was worried that stories denying the existence of these weapons would make the newspaper look "silly" if they were discovered.[28]

The *Post*'s National Security reporter, Dana Priest, also alluded to the public's support for the Bush administration and how it might have impinged on thinking at the newspaper. Kurtz writes that "Priest noted . . . that skeptical stories usually triggered hate mail questioning your patriotism and suggesting that you somehow be delivered into the hands of the terrorists."[29]

Providing an example of the "groupthink" that pervaded the newspaper at the time, Kurtz mentions longtime reporter Walter Pincus' attempts to publish a story casting doubt on the Bush administration's assertion that Saddam Hussein was lying about his weapons programs. Pincus apparently ran into difficulties when discussing the story with editors and it was only at Woodward's insistence that the article was finally printed. Even then the story only appeared on page A17, and followed a series of page 1 articles supporting the administration's viewpoint.[30] In a succinct statement on the *Post*'s war reporting, Downie said that the newspaper often ignored the minority who were criticizing the administration and its rush to war. "We didn't pay enough attention to the minority," Downie said.[31]

Another media organization that followed the *Times* in apologizing was the liberal magazine, *The New Republic*. Having supported the Bush administration's decision to topple Saddam Hussein's regime, the magazine produced a surprising editorial in June 2004 apologizing to its readers for the support given to the administration. "We feel regret, but no shame . . . Our strategic rationale for war has collapsed."[32] According to Kurtz, the decision came after a rancorous editorial meeting. Adding his own apologies to the upwelling of apologetic media, CNN's Tucker Carlson commented, "I am embarrassed that I supported war in Iraq."[33]

Supporting Carlson's feelings, Lesley Stahl, the CBS news correspondent for *60 Minutes* also spoke about her feelings towards a number of stories she had worked on. In particular, she mentioned two reports made before the start of the war that doubted Saddam Hussein had destroyed Iraq's WMD. "I look on those stories as mistakes, journalistic mistakes. . . . I made them, and I regret it."[34]

Speaking to an audience at a high school, Stahl said she remembered a trip to Iraq in October 2003 to interview Iraqi officials, scientists, and military leaders. All those she interviewed told her that Hussein had no contacts with Osama bin Laden and that they were enemies. Stahl said she believed them, but also said she refused to accept their claims that the WMD had been destroyed. Stahl said that at the time everyone was sure that these claims were lies and that Hussein was hiding the weapons somewhere. The *60 Minutes* reporter said that while she regretted her failure, she is not sure what else she could have done.[35]

With the media undergoing a period of lamentation and hand wringing, it is difficult to know what to make of the flurry of apologies regarding news reports published in the days and weeks leading up to the Iraq war. There was, however, a remarkable similarity in the way that the American media behaved over the attacks on September 11; this behavior was exemplified by one of America's most famous journalists: Dan Rather.

TRACING THE APOLOGY ARC

Appearing on the *Late Show with David Letterman* an emotional Dan Rather said, in the days after September 11, "George Bush is the president. He makes the decisions. As just one American, wherever he wants me to line up, just tell me where." By the middle of 2002, nearly a full year after the devastating attacks Rather appeared to have changed his mind about his own response to September 11.

Speaking on a BBC program, Rather commented, "I worry that patriotism run amok will trample the very values that the country seeks to defend." On the subject of patriotism, Rather had this to say, "One finds oneself saying, 'I know the right question but you know what? This is not exactly the right time to ask it.' "[36]

Though personal to him, Rather's words may also be seen as evidence of the extraordinary emotional response that journalists, who are also human beings, had to the horrendous September 11 attacks. First, journalists heavily identified themselves with the public's and the Bush administration's desire to find the perpetrators and bring them to justice. Second, once the passage of time had allowed for a clearer, more impersonal judgment, there was a return to journalistic—as opposed to human—sensibilities; indeed, there was a growing realization among journalists of the important need to uphold balanced and contextualized reporting in the face of a compulsion to report from the Bush administration's perspective.

Seen in these terms, it is tempting to say that, as shown by Rather, it was as if a spell had been lifted from the eyes of journalists, allowing them to return to their daily reporting. This is not to denigrate such a response, as has been mentioned by other media commentators, in terms of size and scale, no other country's media profession has had to deal with such a crisis. The American media were literally in new territory, and while criticism of their response may be warranted, it often comes from those who refuse to accept that similar responses might have been deemed appropriate in their own countries.

The trouble is, while this is entirely plausible for the September 11 attacks, it does not properly excuse the media's behavior during the war in Iraq. After all, as Oscar Wilde wrote in *The Importance of Being Earnest*, "To lose one parent, Mr. Worthing, may be regarded as a misfortune; to lose both looks like carelessness."[37] Why would the media appear to trace the same arc of apparent silence, followed by apologies long after they could influence the course of events? Was it media carelessness or was something else at work?

One of the likely answers is that the events of September 11 continued to exert a tremendous influence on the way the media reported on the war in Iraq. The impulse towards supporting a government in the period leading to war can be extremely strong, and fears over the reaction of the public, based on hard experiences learned after the events of September 11, may have led many media organizations to be cautious when reporting on the Bush administration's justifications for war.

Interestingly, this makes the *Times'* apologia even more significant on the general question of why it failed to report more skeptically. While the *Times* delved into the institutional question of what appeared to go wrong, it does not seem to have answered the wider question of what may have influenced the *Times* to act this way! As a result, there is no connection between the events in this period and the reports appearing in the newspaper. It is almost as if the newspaper believed it was hermetically sealed and therefore safe from the influence of the patriotic environment quelling dissent. The failure to go further than the 1,175 words written on May 26 is unhelpful because it fails to explain the arc that American journalism followed in the period after September 11 and during the war in Iraq.

There are also other questions to be asked of the media who offered apologizes to their audiences. In the case of the *Times*, why did it place its mea culpa on an inside page A10 rather than the front page? The editorial staff at the newspaper must have known that any apology on the subject of the war would be newsworthy and would make headlines around the world, so why negate this newsworthiness to a lesser page making it appear as if their instinct was to hide the review.

After all, the decision of the *Times* was both brave and ethically correct: so why then act as if ashamed of the consequences? Moreover, there is a considerable irony in the fact that one of the accusations was that the newspaper underplayed stories criticizing the Bush administration by placing the stories on the inside pages. Why compound this perception by underplaying the report on why this was done. By doing so, the newspaper, whose instinct had been so good on the need to re-evaluate its journalism, allowed its competitor—the *Washington Post*—whose report came out later, to steal the ethical high ground by placing its own investigation on A01.

There is also the *Times'* lateness in responding to criticism of its reporting. Written over 14 months after the start of the war, the editors' note in the *Times* looks somewhat tardy and gives the impression that either the *Times* was holding onto the note for a sufficiently long time in order to allow the dust to settle, or that the criticism of Jack Shafer, et al., actually forced the *Times* to carry out the review. Either way, the *Times* appeared reactive rather than proactive.

Such a distinction removes some of the shine from the original decision; nevertheless, following on from the Jayson Blair scandal and the self-inflicted wounds of this in-depth review, it was courageous of the newspaper's editorial staff to contemplate going through the same process on an even more contentious subject. This is particularly true given the fact that, as in the Blair case, the outcome was not necessarily that easy to gauge.

Furthermore, the fact that other media organizations also apologized around the same time is continuing proof of the newspaper's ability to set the tone for the media industry as a whole. To a certain extent, the other mea culpas gave cover to the *Times*, giving the impression that the problem was industry wide rather than occurring in certain media organizations.

Was the reporting problem institutional or did it lie with individual reporters or editors? Both the *Times* and the *Post* appear to give credence to the problem being an institutional one. It is significant that while outside media pointed to articles by Judith Miller at the *Times* or, say, Barton Gellman at the *Post* as being the source of the problem, the two newspapers blame editors who were intent on "rushing scoops into the paper" (*Times*), or "underplayed" some stories (the *Post*).[38] This view was supported by editors in charge at the newspapers who refused to blame individual journalists.

The decisions of both Keller and Downie Jr. are probably the right ones: modern journalists may have bylines, but the publishing process of a newspaper rightfully leaves responsibility in the hands of the executive editor and his or her publisher. However, this does not mean that it was only an institutional question. With the advantage of hindsight it does seem that a reporter such as Miller was given too much room in which to maneuver, while journalists who held views contrary to her own found it more difficult to have their stories published in prominent parts of the newspaper.

Furthermore, the real problem seems to be that, while the institution may have been at fault, the pressure on the media as a whole also had a role to play. Patriotism exerts a powerful pull and this was particularly true before the war in Iraq; no wonder then that this influenced the thinking of journalists and editors at newspapers that had fine traditions of resisting government pressures. Such pressures have existed before, but on the questions of WMD they acted as a powerful undercurrent dragging the media in a direction they may not have followed in peacetime.

If an apology indicates a willingness to change! How can the media act to ensure that the failings regarding the war in Iraq are not repeated? How can the media return to the position of holding governments to account when, for a period, they were the unsuspecting conduits through which heavily biased information about Saddam Hussein was foisted on a trusting public? Is there a need for changes that go beyond those already discussed and mooted by media organizations? The answer lies in a reintroduction of the skeptic's test when examining the executive's actions.

Chapter 8

REINTRODUCING THE
SKEPTIC'S TEST

Extraordinary claims require extraordinary proof.
—Carl Sagan

THE JOURNALIST AS SKEPTIC

The following is an examination of what the *Washington Post*'s former ombudsman, Michael Getler has called, "[B]y far the single most important and most disappointing performance by the press, including the *Washington Post*."[1] The failure involved the media's inability to come to grips with a story that, in many ways, asked too much of journalists and editors. It was a story assessing the closed world of national security and calling into question the motives of the executive branch of government that, according to some, pushed too hard for war. As Getler argues, "The key question for journalists is how the process of vetting the main prewar rationale for sending Americans into war took place, or failed to take place."[2]

Alongside Getler's question, there is another question to be asked by the media: What can the media do to avoid a repetition of their failings in the Iraq war? The answer is a complicated one! The media need to return to operating with a healthy skepticism towards the words and deeds of government! The media need to acknowledge that, given their own public interest role, their job is not to confirm the judgments of government where there is no evidence to do so, but to ask hard questions and to pursue those questions until they have answers. Such a proposition involves a return to skepticism; something, which, at times during the lead-up to the Iraq war, it seemed that many journalists had forgotten as they accepted the claims and justifications of government.

Therefore, if the apparent forgetfulness over the need for skepticism is to be reversed and is, instead, to be turned into an act of remembering, a suitable definition of the journalist/skeptic is necessary. Based on the *Oxford English Dictionary*, a skeptic is someone who is inclined to question the truth or soundness of accepted ideas; someone who is critical or who remains incredulous of the words of others. Using the dictionary definition as a foundation, the journalist/skeptic is someone willing to question commonly accepted beliefs, to confront others with alternative views and to provide the fullest possible account of what is happening in any given situation.

Despite heavy criticism of the American media in recent years, it was not so long ago that skepticism of government was a defining feature of a journalist's reporting. This was especially true during the high-water mark of Watergate when journalists represented the public when questioning the motivations of President Richard Nixon and his administration. As Jonathan Keats wrote in October 2003, "[j]ournalists held themselves directly and exclusively responsible to the American people. Nixon, on the contrary, considered the media a piece of machinery built to connect him with his constituency."[3] At that time, the media remained confident about its ability to hold successive administrations to account; however, in the intervening period, the media's confidence appears to have dissipated.

Perhaps, as has been suggested elsewhere in this book, the communications strategy of increasingly sophisticated administrations, as well as rampant commercialization and a hungry eye for profit have undermined the media's ability to act on the American people's behalf. Viewed from this perspective, it was only a matter of time before the media found itself in its present position. Nevertheless, whether this is true or not the storm—in the form of the war in Iraq—has struck, and, if the media are to weather this storm, there is now a need to find safe harbor. With this in mind, the media should acknowledge that, in their relationship with government, the best anchorage is to be found in a return to skeptical journalism.

Some journalists and media commentators echo the need for the profession to return to its grass roots and to be skeptical. Speaking at a debate on media and Iraq, Robert A. Kittle, editorial page editor at the *San Diego Union-Tribune*, said, "In the future, the new media will all be healthily more skeptical than we were. That will serve our readers and viewers a lot better."[4] Appearing to support Kittle, Orville Schell, Dean of the Graduate School of Journalism at UC Berkeley, said of the Iraq war, "[T]here was simply almost no major media outlets being watchdogs, being skeptics, raising the right questions."[5]

Although it seems that the journalism profession is now going through a period of reflection in the United States and there are reporters questioning the media's role in the Iraq war, the thinking on the subject appears to lack cohesion.

The following is an attempt to set out new ways of applying skepticism in the reporting of government—it is in effect, a skeptic's charter. It does not profess to be an exhaustive list, nor has it been written in the hope that it will be adopted; after all, change must come from within media organizations, it cannot be forced from without. Where possible the following sets out a discussion on important areas of journalism, and attempts to provide an answer in line with the practice of skeptical journalism.

WHAT IF THE GOVERNMENT HELD A BACKGROUND BRIEFING AND NO ONE CAME?

The discussion over background briefings should be seen not only through the prism of the Iraq war, but also as a long-running dispute between the media and the executive branch in Washington. Over many years, there have been numerous complaints regarding their use, particularly during the Reagan era, and there have even been half-hearted attempts at boycotts, but they were not successful and on each occasion the media returned to the fold.

The rebellion against background briefings in the 1980s was led by Bill Kovach, the then Washington bureau chief of the *New York Times*. According to Kovach, "A few other reporters joined us at first when we asked briefings be kept open and left the room if they were not. But the support didn't last long." Kovach said the reason "was that [journalists] would surrender their independence if they took part in such group actions."[6]

For government, the background briefing represents an excellent way of delivering information to the White House press corps without having to be responsible for the information. The system makes effective use of the journalists' convention regarding protection of sources and allows government officials to escape censure for their comments. In effect, the background briefing is a secure delivery system for "spin;" it ensures that the government can introduce information into the media sphere without having to go on the record.

Under the Bush administration background briefings have become a way of life, and their continual use during the Iraq war led to the media once again discussing a possible boycott. The problem has been the following: how do you convince high government officials to go on the record, especially when your competitor is perhaps less choosy about his sources. The mainstream media are also bedeviled by a traditional dislike of acting in unison, and the lack of uniformity has caused problems when discussing background briefings with the government who has often exploited the situation.

In reaction to the Bush administration, journalists have started arguing that the best way to reduce the number of background briefings is to refuse to attend. The president and chief executive of the Associated Press, Tom Curley, has argued, "We have to be able to walk out of the room when somebody goes off the record."[7] *Knight Ridder* reporter Ron Hutcheson, president of the White House Correspondents Association, who once carried out a solo protest at a background briefing, argues that it is important to act tough with the administration. "If you push back you get results, and we need to push back collectively." The desire for collective action, however, was not supported in some quarters. In an e-mail on the subject, the *Washington Post's* Executive Editor, Leonard Downie Jr. said, "We just don't believe in unified action...we can't participate in the kind of discussion you are proposing."[8]

While the media often appear to disagree on the solution, there is a strong dislike of the briefings. The *Post*'s White House correspondent Dana Milbank has called them "background noise" and says he cannot remember the last time he used information from such a meeting.[9] The biggest critic of this overused tool is the former public editor to the *New York Times* Daniel Okrent who has called them "an affront to journalistic integrity and an insult to the citizenry."[10] Okrent has also argued that the "big five newspapers in Washington—*USA Today*, the *Wall Street Journal*, the *New York Times*, the *Washington Post* and the *Los Angeles Times*—[should] walk out of anonymous briefings."[11] "At a time when news organizations have real credibility problems, to invite more by taking part in this charade is intellectually dishonest and cowardly," wrote Okrent.[12]

In early 2005, there were serious attempts by the media to get the Bush administration to rein in its efforts to feed the media information anonymously. The *New York Times'* Washington bureau chief, Philip Taubman, informed his staff, via an e-mail, that the *Times* was part of a consortium of newspapers that were attempting to force the administration to rethink its policy. The policy brought a swift response from the then White House spokesperson, Scott McClellan, who said that he would be happy to end the briefings so long as the media ended its use of anonymous sources. Speaking to *Editor and Publisher*, McClellan said, ''I told them upfront that I would be first to sign on if we could get an end to the use of anonymous sources in the media.''[13]

Faced with an intransigent administration linking the question of background briefings to the use of confidential sources, it was obvious the media's somewhat halfhearted rebellion would lead nowhere. No one appears to have recognized McClellan's precarious position; after all, it was often Bush administration officials who were demanding the confidentiality, so they could pursue the administration's policies. Nevertheless, despite this apparent air of hypocrisy, the President's White House spokesperson was allowed to have the final say on the matter.

In an article titled, ''Stop Us Before We're Briefed Again,'' Professor of Journalism at New York University, Jay Rosen, also criticized the media for not realizing that the power to control the situation was actually in their own hands. As Rosen pointed out, rather than politely asking the Bush administration to stop using the briefings, the media could actually stop attending them, therefore sending a powerful signal regarding its feelings on the subject.

Rosen writes:

> But realize that another course of action is available. (Maybe you do and are not talking about it.) Withdraw from the background game entirely by changing your policy unilaterally, and as part of a move to raise transparency overall. Explain it that way to your readers. Tell them that while it may mean some stories and insights go missing, the benefits of ending your participation in a stealth practice far outweigh those losses.[14]

Rosen's view is similar to Okrent's, but, sadly, the media mostly ignored them. Instead, the media seem to have ceded control to the Bush administration and, while on occasion, it has relented and provided the media with proper on-the-record briefings, the situation remains the same. As a result, the failure is largely that of the media's and it is worth mentioning that the fault lies with some media organizations who believe that joint actions lead to a loss of individual control. The supposed loss of individualism is negligible when compared to the death-by-a-thousand-drips of a newspaper's credibility, as it continually apologizes to its audience for its news reporting. A newspaper lives by its reputation and an open invitation to the administration into a newspaper's pages through the unchecked channel of background briefings is damaging to the newspaper. Seen from this perspective, joint action was not only necessary; it was also the only means of forcefully representing the media's views.

For these reasons, the *Post*'s views on the subject are disappointing because it refuses to acknowledge that all of the media face the same problem and that joint action offered the only chance of success against a strong administration. This is particularly true when considering what the administration would do if the "Big Five" stopped attending the briefings! Without these powerful media organizations, the Bush administration would have been forced to reach out to smaller media; in the past, it has shown just such an inclination, but the absence of the five newspapers would have had a considerable impact on the thinking of other media.

Given the primary position of newspapers such as the *Washington Post*, the *New York Times*, and the *Los Angeles Times*, it is very likely that other media organizations would have followed suit. Many other media organizations across the United States depend on the "Big Five" organizations for their views and opinions, and they may even wait for these newspapers to report before covering the same subject. Moreover, the Bush administration would not have been able to use the remaining media in the same way; their audiences are smaller and narrower.

There is also the audience to be considered! Even readers of smaller, more local newspapers, deserve to know who is delivering their information to them. It is likely that the boycott by the "Big Five" would have led to discussion in the local newspapers, and many of these media organizations would have joined the boycott. Therefore, rather than concerning itself with the loss of individual choice, the *Washington Post* should have considered its position in light of what was best for its readers. Fears for the loss of individualism are also strange when acknowledging that, in the past, the media has worked together on joint trade union struggles or First Amendment issues. Significantly, many of the "Big Five" newspapers have fought bitter battles with trade unions and yet they appeared to hesitate when the opponent was the government!

Rather than asking the Bush administration to solve the problem, the media should have banded together and demanded changes. Okrent and Rosen were correct, the media had the power to solve the situation themselves, and they should have exercised it. Where the Bush administration tried to foist unattributable information on the media, journalists should either have refused to attend or have walked out after failing to get the officials to agree to speak on the record.

After all, such action was always worth considering because it was such a high stakes game. As mentioned in so many briefs to the courts, the media play a watchdog role within society and they have a duty to act in the public's interest. But, the media cannot have it both ways; they cannot assert this right before the courts when seeking the cover of the First Amendment and yet deny this role when seeking to exercise their commercial and business duties: namely to increase sales.

Obviously, it is understandable that questions of competition and commercialism arise when journalists are chasing stories or seeking the help of the Bush administration to file a story; however, a news story should not be pursued to the detriment of the public's right to know who is providing their news and information. The hunt for an important story cannot be allowed to trump the media's duty to the public.

In many ways, it appears that the media have forgotten this duty and it has damaged them. Concerns over where the media obtain their information flow into overall concerns about the media's credibility. The *Washington Post* might assert the need for the preservation of its independence, but how much weight does this carry when balanced against the public's rights? There are similar problems with the media's general approach to sources.

OFF THE RECORD, BUT IN THE PAPER

According to a survey sponsored by the Associated Press Managing Editors National Credibility Roundtables project, which saw 35 news organizations gather 11,611 reader responses in 42 states, 44 percent of the respondents said they were less likely to believe a story if it contained an anonymous source. To provide an industry view, 419 editors were also asked their opinions about anonymous sources and while most news organizations allow anonymous sources to be used, almost one-quarter of editors had banned their use because of fears over credibility.[15]

One of the readers participating in the survey made perhaps the best comment, "Anonymous sources should be considered the journalistic equivalent of the 'nuclear option'; . . . [i]f the information provided cannot be independently verified, it cannot and should not be used. The standard of verification must be set much higher for anonymous sources than that used for open sources, as the risks associated with error are so much higher."[16] The problem with this view is that while such sources might be considered to be the media's nuclear option, even a cursory reading shows that many of the best newspapers in the United States are engaged in nuclear proliferation: anonymous sources are literally everywhere.

Once again, Okrent is far ahead of the pack when he states, "there is nothing more toxic to responsible journalism than an anonymous source" and that the newspaper's defense that it is engaged in reporting and not confirming stories is little more than "a license granted to liars."[17] The question of the use of anonymous sources is at the heart of the reporting in the lead-up to the war in Iraq because, like the background briefing, it is yet another delivery system for injecting highly controversial and contested assertions directly into the public's bloodstream. Reporters at the *Post* and the *Times* repeatedly used such sources to bolster their reports, adding crucial quotes from intelligent sources and White House officials who did not wish to be named.

Unfortunately, for the most part, such sources were wrong and yet their agreements with the media held fast and they were not exposed for being incorrect. One of the interesting comments by Okrent is that journalists who are lied to, as appeared to have happened during the war in Iraq, should not be bound by their duty of confidentiality; the journalists' duty to their newspaper and their readers would require them, if necessary, to expose the fraudulent source to the world. As Okrent succinctly puts it, "information does not earn immunity."

Sometime after the Iraq invasion, the *Times* conducted reviews of their rules on the use of anonymous sources. Published in February 2004, the *Times* said the use of "unidentified sources is reserved for situations in which the newspaper could not otherwise print information it considers reliable and newsworthy...and we accept an obligation not only to convince a reader of their reliability, but also to convey what we can learn of their motivation[.]"[18] The review provided an examination of the principles for granting anonymity and called for an investigation into whether the source had first-hand knowledge of the facts.

The review also sets out the role and duties of editors at the *Times*: "Any editor who learns a source's identity is required to maintain exactly the same confidentiality as the reporter. That editor may not divulge the identity to other reporters, or to unauthorized editors. And the editor may not use the source—either for reporting on the current story or for later ones."[19] Significantly, the review also states, the "reporter and source must understand that the commitment [to anonymity] is undertaken by the newspaper[.]"[20]

With regard to the process of accepting an anonymous source, the *Times'* assertion that it is the newspaper which undertakes the commitment is important. When looking at the question of sources over the period from Watergate to Judith Miller's reporting of the Iraq war, it is hard to accept that the newspaper was always in charge of the process. While *Post* executive editor, Ben Bradlee, knew the name of the "deep throat" source, journalist Bob Woodward often appeared to be in control; significantly, the Watergate case shows the journalists controlling the issue of sources; always working one step ahead of the editors and the newspaper. The same can be said of Judith Miller at the *Times* where she was given considerable autonomy. Unfortunately, for the *Times*, some of Miller's sources were discredited which, in turn, undermined the newspaper and its editors who were often perceived as ineffectual.

The *Times'* attempt to wrestle control from the journalist is a laudatory outcome of the war in Iraq, but, in real terms, it is not necessarily so easy to put those words into practice. Given a newspaper's output, and the time pressure, it is hard to believe that it will have sufficient numbers of staff to maintain a continuous review of its use of sources. Newspapers are fiefdoms and those in control take their positions very seriously: will journalists be so ready to give up the names of sources to junior editors? How can editors control so-called "star" journalists who, like Miller, can often operate in a vacuum outside of normal constraints?

Perhaps motivated by competition with the *Times*, the *Post* also sought to revise its rules on sources. The *Post* states that it has a preference for sources willing to go on the record and calls for editors and reporters to attempt to give readers as much information about the source as possible. Editors are also seen as important in the process and, as Downie Jr. writes, the goal is to "publish stories that are accurate and complete" during a period where "Internet-borne rumors, talk show speculation and sophisticated spinning by newsmakers who want to influence how the news is reported while hiding their responsibility for doing so."[21] Michael Getler, added his own views in an article written in the *Post* on October 9, 2005. Discussing Iraq, the *Post's* outgoing ombudsman said that editors were often the weak link and that it was their job to set the tone and provide direction for journalists. To do this, "They should be experienced and as informed as reporters."[22]

Like the *Times*, the *Post* appears to point towards the editorial process as being pivotal in the use of anonymous sources. Another factor, and one raised by Jack Shafer at *Slate* magazine, is the possibility that it is the tradition of shackling journalists to facts that necessitates anonymous sources. In Shafer's view, the continuous need to support facts with quotes creates news that relies on "a stenographic procession of facts, quotations, and official denials," which not only makes many articles repetitive, but also fails to inform the reader.

As a rebuttal to this type of journalism, Shafer calls for journalists to be allowed to introduce their own voice to the article by "asserting what they know to be true" and to include analysis.[23] The idea is an original one and it leans towards a more European style of news writing, but it would merely exchange one set of problems for another. In particular, like European journalism, the change in stance would produce both good and bad journalism and would lead to problems in the American media with regard to the strict separation of news and opinion. Would there perhaps be a deep pause at the end of an article, while the journalist gathered his thoughts and went on to say, "What follows is what I know to be true." Is there a difference between what a journalist "knows" ("Assertion of fact") and what he "believes" to be true ("Opinion")? How would readers distinguish the two and would they appreciate the nuances?

Obviously, while some journalists might spurn their use, anonymous sources are an important asset when following stories involving national security. It is also doubtful whether anyone wishes to see a blanket ban on their use, but there is an acknowledgment that they have caused the media considerable problems. How is it possible to regain the balance and perhaps encourage greater audience confidence? The answer perhaps lies in attempting to restrict their use to the occasions when they are actually needed.

The first step must be to redress the imbalance allowed to grow in the newsroom where journalists orbiting in the firmament have been allowed to operate without proper checks and balances from editors. Journalists are important, but it is the newspaper that people purchase. Where necessary some journalists should be reminded of this. They should also be reminded that the role of an editor is vital in the production of good news and that journalists are responsible for submitting their work for appropriate checks.

Publishers and executive editors need to come together to create an environment where no editor is fearful of what will happen if he questions a stellar journalists' work. In relation to sources, journalists have to accept that the source is not theirs, but the newspaper's and for this reason there is a need for others to be involved in the assessment of whether it is right or wrong to allow a source to be used in a particular article. This is not a move to force journalists to give up their sources, but both journalists and their sources must become more accountable to their newspapers.

In the interests of accountability, newspapers should also maintain a system of continuous review of sources and their veracity. In large organizations, it might even be necessary to employ a "sources editor" for the sole purpose of maintaining information on sources, as well as developing fresh ways of dealing with what has become a difficult problem. The purpose of such a role is not to express a distrust of journalists, but to ensure that publishers and editors have a greater appreciation of what is being done in the newspaper's name.

The reality is that the use of anonymous sources has to be scaled back. They have to be used sparingly. A failure to resist the urge to use such sources will only lead the public to believe that newspapers, and other media, lack credibility. It has often been said by editors defending anonymous sources that they do not necessarily agree with the statements made by the sources. After the war in Iraq, this can no longer be used as an excuse; if the media seek to hold the government to account they must also hold themselves to account. Newspapers like the *Times* and the *Post*, as well as news agencies and broadcasters realize this, and they have made a start. Other media in the United States should also accept their conclusions.

VERIFICATION, VERIFICATION, VERIFICATION

Journalism is not only about reporting the facts; it is about developing ways to ensure that those facts have a basis in reality. During the war in Iraq, and especially in the lead-up beforehand, many media organizations appeared to have an undue belief in the veracity of the Bush administration's statements. Such unwarranted belief tainted the reporting on the Iraq war, and eventually undermined the credibility of the news organizations themselves.

Many of these failings are present in the media's reporting of the speech made by Secretary of State Colin Powell on February 5 before the United Nations Security Council. In reporting Powell's words, much of the media treated them as facts and not as disputed assertions on a topic where there was very little agreement. For example, speaking on CNN *Live Today* on February 6, commentator William Schneider stated, "No one disputes the findings Powell presented at the U.N. that Iraq is essentially guilty of failing to disarm."[24] However, Powell's claims were unverified and, yet, the media appeared to report with little regard for this fine distinction.

Supporting his comments about the failure of the Iraqi government to disarm, and to prove that the country was hoarding chemical weapons, Powell showed dramatic photographs of supposed weapons dumps. He also played audiotapes, gained from the intelligence services, of members of the Iraqi armed forces discussing the need to "sanitize communications."[25] The media dutifully reported these statements as if they were accepted facts. In *60 Minutes II*, on the same day as the Powell speech, Dan Rather said, "Holding a vial of anthrax-like powder, Powell said Saddam might have tens of thousands of liters of anthrax. He showed how Iraqi jets could spray that anthrax and how mobile laboratories are being used to concoct new weapons."[26]

In other cases, the media failed to follow up on the progress of the U.N. weapons inspectors and to contrast these with the statements made by the Bush administration, or they failed to return to a story to question the original assertions when new information was at hand. The result was that the media allowed a number of key assertions to stand when at best they were questionable and at worst untrue.

In October 2002, the Central Intelligence Agency (CIA) issued a warning that Iraq was restarting its nuclear weapons program at Al-Tuwaitha, a site formerly used for Iraq's nuclear weapons program. But, these claims were proved to be unfounded when, in December of the same year, the U.N. weapons inspectors returned to Iraq and inspected the site. During their inspection they found no evidence that supported the CIA claim, which, in turn, had been used by President Bush in his speech in Cincinnati on October 7. Much of the media, however, reported the initial claims without explaining that they were not proven facts. Some media then compounded the problem by failing to set the record straight once they did have information disproving the CIA's claim.

On the subject of Powell's presentation, a U.N. coordinator for Iraq, Hans von Sponeck told the British *Mirror* newspaper, "The inspectors have found nothing which was in the Bush and Blair dossiers of last September. What happened to them? They are totally embarrassed by them. I have seen facilities in pieces in Iraq which U.S. intelligence reports say are dangerous."[27]

Although the term "stenographers for the government" is a much abused term for the way the media reported on the war in Iraq, it is true to say that there were times when the media reported in such a way that they supported the aims and ambitions of the Bush administration. This is largely because some elements of the media accepted as truth many of the assertions made by officials in the Bush administration. There was often a failure to hold them up to the harsh light of verification. Rather than wait until these claims could be verified, some media went ahead and reported them as truth. Instead of accepting claims at face value, the media should have distinguished between claims made by the Bush administration and what could be proven.

To make this distinction, the media needed to ask itself whether the assertions being made could be verified by independent sources; if not, the statements of officials should have been cast in such a way as to inform the reader that they were not to be treated as truth. There is no doubt that such journalism is extremely difficult in circumstances where there are deadlines and the threat of being "scooped" by competitors is a reality. To the media's credit, there were organizations that achieved this, but they were often few and far between when compared to the chorus of other organizations who failed to apply skepticism to the Bush administration's claims.

In trying to understand this situation, it is worth considering a hypothetical news organization that works in accordance with the strict standards of the rules of legal evidence, rather than the rules of journalism. In such an organization, the evidentiary rules would have called on the journalists to advance only what they know to be true. To state what they know to be provable. There would have been a burden of proof: an exacting standard that would have to be met in order for a news story to be published. To achieve this, each link of the evidentiary chain would be tested, with some links discarded while others supported by fresh investigations. This did not happen in some media organizations who appeared to forget that it is better to be late but right, rather than early and wrong.

In an article appearing at the Journalism.org website for the Project for Excellence in Journalism titled, "Developing Methods of Verification," there are six rules for the purposes of verification: never add anything that was not there, never deceive the audience, apply the rules of transparency, be transparent when dealing with sources, rely on your own reporting, and keep an open mind.[28] These are important rules for journalists and if they are added to the notion that important stories should be developed at a slower pace, in ignorance of the competition, and that the media should always be skeptical when dealing with the claims of government, they might improve the standards of journalism in media organizations.

DEVELOPING EDITORIAL VIGILANCE
AND INDEPENDENCE

Writing in the *Toronto Globe and Mail*, Editor-in-Chief Ed Greenspon, when asked about investigative journalism said, "Reporters need to be courageous and vigilant. Editors need to be vigilant and courageous."[29] The need for editors to display vigilance about how stories are being shaped by journalists is essential. Editors need to be in a position to give advice, as well as to challenge a journalist's own perception of his or her story. The creation of a newspaper story often occurs because of the tensions between editors and journalists.

The problem with some of the reporting on the Iraq war was that some journalists managed to escape this rigorous form of due diligence. At the *Times*, journalists, such as Judith Miller, were given greater leeway; whereas at the *Post*, it appeared that editors failed to give credence to stories not supporting the assertions of the Bush administration. As a consequence, in both cases, the outcome was that the story of the decision to go to war was unbalanced and out of kilter.

To bring reporting back to the central ground of neutrality, editors need to assert themselves again, but they need to do so based on their willingness to remain skeptical of the stories that are being brought back to the office by their journalists. The usurpation of the editor's role within a media organization, particularly a newspaper, has come about because some journalists are now considered to have greater weight than others. In reporting the decision to go to war, it is those journalists, with their contacts within the administration, who are going to be viewed as the most powerful—even by their publishers. Journalists are extremely secretive about their sources, often for good reason because the relationship is based on trust, but if editors are going to be kept out of the decision-making process, news stories will suffer because the means to critically examine a news story will have been degraded.

Veteran editor Reid MacCluggage has termed the process of good editing "prosecutorial editing." According to MacCluggage the term means, "to challenge information reporters bring back to the newspaper, and to question conclusions drawn from that information. It's our job to battle assumptions or preconceived notions and provide scrutiny needed to make certain that all stories are fair and accurate."[30] MacCluggage also says that, in the same way lawyers are trained in cross-examination, editors should be trained in the ability to strip a story down and to "[e]xpose its weaknesses."[31]

Publishers and executive editors have to support their junior and senior editors in turf battles with journalists over the question of access to sources and the questioning of stories. If the skeptical journalist is to return, editors need to work without fear that their decisions will be second guessed by journalists capable of complaining straight to the executive editor or even the publisher. It is important for newspapers to appreciate that, no matter how successful, star journalists are subordinate to the newspaper's desire to get the facts right and inform their readership. After the Iraq war, the heads of media organisations should be asking themselves the following question regarding news reporting where does the balance of power lie within their media organization and does it need to be adjusted?

If there are difficulties then the management should start to consider adjustments and the most likely place to start is within the editorial section. A failure to make these adjustments can lead to the types of crises that have haunted the media over the last few years, especially over its Iraq reporting. Journalists are of vital importance to a media organization, but publishers or executive editors will not be aware of what is happening beneath them if they do not empower their editors to operate confidently and independently.

IGNORING THE PATRIOTIC BACKGROUND NOISE!

When commenting on the performance of the media in the war in Iraq, former *Washington Post* ombudsman, Michael Getler, said that some of the editors "didn't have their eye on, and didn't go for, the right ball at the right time."[32] Seeking an explanation for this he says, "Some journalists or news organizations may have been intimidated by the atmosphere."[33] Getler's words are an acknowledgment of the media's difficulty reporting about government during a war; especially when the public is fully supportive and is likely to turn on organizations that criticize the executive.

The pressures on the media have also been articulated by *New York Times* correspondent Elisabeth Bumiller who, in answer to criticism of the media's failure to hold the president to account during a March 20, 2003 press conference, told the *Baltimore Sun*:

> I think we were very deferential because in the East Room press conference it's live. It's very intense. It's frightening to stand up there. I mean think about it, you're standing on prime time television asking the President of the United States a question and when the country is about to go to war. There

was a very serious, somber tone that evening and I think it made, you know, nobody wanted to get into an argument with the president at this serious time. It had a very heavy feeling of history to it, that press conference.

Bumiller's words are an admission that in the presence of the president the media suffer from the journalist's equivalent of the Stockholm syndrome when hostages sympathize with their captors. Irrespective of whether the moment is likely to be one of history, it is the job of Bumiller, her newspaper, and the other journalists with her to ensure that the president justifies his decision to go to war. The press conference was not the time for a reflection on the historical moment and to allow the Bush administration to escape from being held accountable. Bumiller's comments are indicative of a lingering belief by some journalists that the government really does know best and that, in time of war, the media's role is simply to report what is said, but not to involve itself in asking important questions.

Of course it must be nerve wracking to question the president on live television, but that is Bumiller's job and it is one that she should not seek to evade. If difficult questions are to be asked of an administration, journalists must set aside their fear of being caught on the wrong side of public opinion—they must ignore the background noise of patriotism—and they should stop being overly deferential to the president and senior officials. Naturally, this does not mean being disrespectful to the president and his appointees, but it does mean asking hard questions to all public servants. Once again the key is skepticism about the claims of government.

SLOWING DOWN THE MEDIA ORGANIZATION'S "METABOLISM"

On taking over the executive editorship of the *New York Times* Howell Raines famously announced that he intended to raise the "competitive metabolism" of the newspaper. While Raines' idea made sense in terms of continuing the *Times*'s fine tradition of being the newspaper of record and the first to break a news story, on the question of Iraq, the desire to be first often seemed to prevent the newspaper from gaining an overview of what was actually happening.

Significantly, it often appeared that the newspaper's reporting, especially about WMD, was enthused with a competitive desire to be the first media organization to trumpet new information. As Daniel Okrent has argued, the *Times'* desire to be first seemed to overwhelm the desire to be right in the news reporting, and while it is important that newspapers beat their competitors it can undermine the culture and the procedures introduced to ensure that the newspaper also gets its facts correct.

Okrent believes that war stories require a higher standard of care than normal stories and he is right to highlight the need for extra vigilance when dealing with intelligence-led stories. This duty often seemed to be set aside as the media settled into its own battle to be the first to break stories. There is now a need to reflect on that battle and for media organizations to consider whether, in future stories involving war and intelligence, it would be better to slow down rather than speed up.

WHAT'S WRONG WITH SAYING, "WE DON'T KNOW?"

There is no doubt that the story of a war is complicated and that it makes demands on journalists and journalism unlike any other story. For much of the lead-up to the war in Iraq, it appeared that the news media were keeping up with the fast-paced story and that, through their many sources, they were providing their audiences with an in-depth analysis of what was happening. Such a view of the media's role has now largely turned out to be false, the media, like the Bush administration, knew very little. The many assertions about Iraq's WMD, including its nuclear weapons program, were erroneous and misleading.

Sadly, the media played a role in regurgitating these facts and communicating them to the American public. Although it is difficult to say that the media helped to convince the American public of the necessity of invading Iraq, there is no doubt that it played a role, no matter how minor. How did the media come to peddle stories that were deeply flawed? Why did they fail to inform their audience that, on certain subjects, they were unsure of the truth? The answer is that the media are not always comfortable with stating that they do not know something.

Given the competitive nature of the media industry, news organizations are used to being in one of two positions: ahead of the news pack chasing the story or in the pack chasing the media organization that broke the story. As a consequence, there is too much focus on keeping ahead or catching-up! However, there is an alternative to either of these accepted positions, namely an organization willing to admit to its audience that, in terms of its present reporting of the story, it simply does not know. The honest approach of admitting you do not know is a far superior approach to the perpetual reporting of what others claim to know, but the media cannot prove!

Honesty in reporting is a much-underestimated means of retaining your audience's respect. The question of WMD deserved more than the traditional approach of "he said/she said," which leaves the reader with the inevitable impression that two sides of any view are of equal value. Media reporting needed to inject a heavy dose of reality into these stories, in fact, they needed to be upfront and honest about what they knew or claimed to know. In essence, the audience deserved to know when the media organization felt it had little or no information to prove what was being asserted.

It is worth repeating that the changes mentioned above can only come from within a media organization. Ultimately, the personnel in a media organization are responsible to themselves, they are the ones who can reshape the newsroom after there have been damaging failings. However, even if every other idea is rejected, the media must accept that, after the Iraq war, there is now a desperate need for the media to escape the gravitational pull of patriotism and to reassert their skepticism about the claims of government: A failure to do so will mean that the executive branch will continue to win the battle over information during wartime and the media will continue to lose credibility.

CONCLUSION

Everyone is entitled to his own opinion, but not his own facts.
—Senator Daniel Patrick Moynihan

STANDING ON THE EDGE

There can be no doubt that, in the Iraq War, the American media faced
one of its greatest trials since the Vietnam War and the Watergate scandal
of the 1970s. The sheer scale of events stretched media organizations to
their limits and placed journalists under enormous pressure as they
attempted to report on the unfolding story.

Unfortunately, while the American media excelled at reporting the
narrative and the chronology of these events, they were unable to fully
investigate the Bush Administration's justifications for war. In consequence, the American media failed in the role envisaged by the framers
of the Constitution; namely, to hold the administration to account for its
actions and to ask, on behalf of the American people, the tough questions
that needed to be asked when a government decides to take its country
to war.

Why did this happen? Why did a media that had questioned the war of a
previous era and confidently exposed the wrongdoing of a president fail in
the attempt to show that there was a credibility gap between the reality of
Iraq and the claims of the Bush administration? The answer is not necessarily reducible to a single set of bold facts, but, instead, should be seen as

a combination of distinct pressures impacting upon the media, both before and during the Iraq war.

The crucial pressures on the media were: First, the climate of patriotism after the September 11 attacks and before the Iraq war, which was subtly manipulated by the Bush administration to suppress dissent; second, the Bush administration's own view of the media as little more than an information delivery system, rather than a constitutionally protected institution with a settled role to play within American society; third, the difficulty of reporting on intelligence issues when the media have no access to the original source; fourth, the heavy politicization of facts and the fracturing of bipartisanship in American politics; and, finally, media scandals that undermined the media's own credibility before the public, matched by a growing commercialization of news that is slowly breaking down the barriers between news and entertainment.

Since September 11, there has been a growing intolerance of dissent and an increase in patriotism. These expressions of patriotism reached their height in the days and weeks after the attacks. During this period, journalists such as Dan Guthrie and Tom Gutting lost their jobs for writing critical pieces about President Bush, while others, such as Bill Maher, found that their comments elicited strong reactions from the public and the Bush administration alike. Maher would later see his show, *Politically Incorrect*, deserted by affiliates and sponsors, and eventually taken off the air by ABC. The environment at the time can best be summed up by the then Presidential spokesperson's response to Bill Maher's comments that the September 11 terrorists were not cowardly. Speaking at a press conference, Fleischer said, "[it's] a terrible thing to say...[Maher's comments are] reminders to all Americans that they need to watch what they say, watch what they do. This is not a time for remarks like that; there never is."

Fleischer's comments were an indication of the Bush administration's own reaction to dissent and for journalists it was a clear warning that, for the period after the attacks, dissent and criticism were to be set aside in favor of whole hearted support for a government forced to confront a new and deadly terrorist threat.

Having weakened the impetus towards dissent, the Bush administration then set about changing the working environment for journalists. The Clinton administration's more open approach to the Freedom of Information Act (FOIA) was reversed by then Attorney General John Ashcroft who informed government departments that his office would support refusals to supply information; there were discussions about the formation of a Pentagon department to inject propaganda into foreign news outlets; broadcasters were approached and invited to stop showing the video tapes supplied by bin Laden and al Qaeda; and the Voice of America faced pressure from the state department over its decision to interview Taliban leader Mullah Omar.

Such events laid the foundation for a new media environment before and during the Iraq war. Although the open space in which the media worked widened somewhat as the United States gained distance from the appalling events of September 11, this space closed once again as the drums beat for war in Iraq. The result was a return to an environment where the media found it easier (and personally safer) to merely report the events as they happened rather than pursue stories that confronted the Bush administration's statements about the need for war.

As had happened previously, the Bush administration and its supporters responded to any form of criticism by calling on the need for security and questioning the patriotism of critics. In September 2002, the House Majority Leader, Tom DeLay said of the Bush administration's critics, ''They will do anything, spend all the time and resources they can, to avoid confronting evil.'' On a plane with journalists, Defense secretary Donald Rumsfeld, also let it be known that he considered criticism of the administration to aid terrorists. Rumsfeld said criticism led to ''more recruiting ... that leads to more encouragement, or that leads to more staying power. Obviously, that makes it more difficult.''

The comments made by the Bush administration's supporters narrowed the scope for debate about the war and challenged the media's role of holding government to account. They also communicated a message to others in American society, especially within the private sphere, who amplified these comments and turned them into specific actions.

In late March 2003, the Al-Jazeera news organization was told by the New York Stock Exchange (NYSE) that it could no longer report from the NYSE's building. While this decision was eventually overturned after considerable international protest, it was a clear sign that where government was prepared to go, the private sphere was often prepared to follow. In San Francisco, journalist Henry Norr of the *San Francisco Chronicle* was dismissed for protesting the war, while Brent Flynn, a columnist for the Star Community Newspaper Group, lost his job after attending an anti-war march. In one of the most explicit cases, *Huron Daily Tribune* journalist Kurt Hauglie resigned after one of his columns criticizing the war was spiked by an editor who feared it would upset the newspaper's readership.

On the Internet, Yellowtimes.org was briefly closed down by its Internet Service Provider (ISP) for showing pictures of American fatalities and there were pressures on Hollywood stars such as Martin Sheen who vigorously protested against the war. Perhaps the worst decision made by a broadcaster was CBS's decision to hold back on the publication of pictures showing the abuse of Iraqi prisoners at the hands of American soldiers. The decision came after the Pentagon warned the broadcaster that such pictures might inflame tensions in Iraq. Given the importance of the story, CBS's decision was a blatant disregard for objective and independent news reporting.

While many of these censorious acts were at arm's length from the government, it is hard not to see them as part of the environment created by the Bush administration. These acts point to a subtle manipulation of the media environment by calling on the public's patriotism and making commercial enterprises extremely nervous about the impact of unpopular dissent on share prices. The comments by the Bush administration also encouraged a strong conservative media that channeled the public's displeasure at dissent and unleashed it on the media. As a result, in late 2002 and early 2003, journalists began to feel extremely uncomfortable about taking on the Bush administration.

The manipulation of the media environment, therefore, contained three vital elements: comments by senior administration officials showing that dissent is unpatriotic; mobilization of the public's support for those comments; and pressure on journalists from other elements of the media and private commerce to support the administration's actions. However, adding to these pressures, and perhaps for the first time in the history of the United States, the Bush administration also sharply questioned the media's role within American society: A tactical decision that further damaged the media's ability to challenge government.

President Bush's admission to a journalist that he disputes the idea that the media reflects what the public is thinking is prejudicial to the media's role. Although it is not necessarily wrong to confront the media's own assumptions about itself, when this comment is seen in conjunction with the comments of other senior Bush administration officials, such as Andrew Card, who is on record as saying he does not believe the media have a check and balance function, it is disturbing. Accepting these comments at face value, it would appear that before and during the Iraq war the Bush administration either sought to use the mainstream media as an information delivery system or simply bypassed them altogether.

The *Washington Post*'s Dana Milbank has first hand experience of the Bush administration's attitude towards the media. Attempts by senior administration officials to have him removed from his White House reporter's position displayed a deep-seated desire to control and influence the way in which the media write about the policies of the executive branch of government. Jonathan Weisman, also a *Washington Post* journalist, revealed his own difficulties when trying to write a story. His experience shows that the Bush administration was prepared to override a journalist's independence in order to have the final word on an article. Concerns about an administration's image are not necessarily new, but the present White House has taken these concerns to new extremes.

During his terms of office, President Bush has also shown a marked reluctance to face the mainstream media. From the start of his first term to January 1, 2004, President Bush gave only 11 solo press conferences and this compares unfavorably with other presidents such as Richard Nixon and Bill Clinton, who gave 23 and 38 respectively. Both the president and the White House's image are heavily guarded and the administration has tried to ensure that its message, and not the media's interpretation, reaches the public. Throughout its terms in office the Bush administration has largely won this information battle and has successfully held much of the mainstream media at bay.

These influences played a considerable part in hindering the reporting of the Iraq war as journalists found it difficult to find officials willing to speak in their own names. For this reason dissent about the war tended to be expressed through anonymous sources in articles where they were pitted against comments made by named administration officials. These anonymous quotes not only failed to carry weight, but also gave the impression they were to be distrusted. Elsewhere, the Bush administration has revealed its skepticism of the mainstream media by reaching over their heads to local media in an attempt to avoid what officials have come to see as the filters of information. Against the most disciplined administration in the history of American politics, the media has found it exceptionally difficult to find information that would have provided balance and contrast to its statements about Iraq.

Concerns about balance and access to information were especially important when the media tried to examine the truth of whether Iraq had WMD, including a nuclear weapons program, which were used by the administration to justify the need for war.

Speaking to the media on September 8, 2002, then national security advisor, Condoleezza Rice, said, in answer to a question about the uncertainty of whether Iraq was pursuing nuclear weapons, "The problem here is that there will always be some uncertainty about how quickly he can acquire nuclear weapons, but we don't want the smoking gun to be a mushroom cloud." Her words followed comments by other officials, including President Bush, on a similar theme and they represented the high-water mark for the Bush administration's arguments for war.

Such comments, however, outlined a scenario that was simply not possible given that Iraq's nuclear weapons program had been successfully dismantled after the first Iraq war in the 1990s. For this reason, the words were little more than scaremongering as the administration tried to push the public towards accepting the necessity for war.

Faced with an administration that appeared to be asserting claims about WMD based on top secret intelligence reports, journalists and editors often fell back on reporting quotes rather than their analysis. While the accusation of being "stenographers" for the Bush administration is trite, comments about mushroom clouds placed the media in a considerable dilemma. Although it was impossible to ignore these comments, because they were often made in keynote speeches, the media found it difficult to investigate them. When reporting these events, the alternative comments of someone like Hans Blix weighed lightly against the comments of the president or his national security advisor.

In truth, the comments about weapons programs were often impossible to challenge. After all, Iraq was a country run by a dictatorship with a long history of deceit, and journalists were not always to simply travel to Iraq to test the claims; nor could they able find members of the U.S. intelligence community willing to speak on the record about whether the claims reflected intelligence reports on these matters. For this reason, the media was largely left out in the cold with little to do, but report the statements of the Bush administration. By doing so, the media was essentially communicating the Bush administration's own message: Iraq is a dangerous country, there is a possibility of a nuclear attack and the United States must act accordingly. This message was communicated to the American people unfiltered and it resonated so deeply that the media must accept some responsibility for the misunderstandings and misconceptions seen in the numerous polls taken over this period.

Some of the media's own reporting in Iraq during the war also appeared to support these claims, and it was published and broadcast with little attempt by editors, publishers, and producers to provide balance and context. Judith Miller of the *New York Times* has taken the blame for much of this reporting. But, in reality, what can a lone journalist like Miller be blamed for? To accept that she managed single handedly to co-opt one of the best newspapers in the world to the will of the Bush administration simply beggars belief!

The *Times'* Executive Editor, Bill Keller, is right to highlight "institutional failure": Miller's reporting escaped the rigorous examination that it warranted and there was a need for senior editors to take up the concerns of more junior editors working with the investigative journalist. Miller, however, was not the only journalist and other media suffered from the overzealous reporting of just one side of the Iraq story. The problem was one that permeated throughout the media and Judith Miller has become the scapegoat for a profession that, at the time, refused to ask deeply uncomfortable questions about its own reporting standards.

Reporting on the Iraq war was not the media's only problem. As well as covering difficult and complicated stories, some media organizations were also wracked by scandals that had a direct bearing on their ability to report. Scandals such as the ones involving Jayson Blair and Jack Kelley undermined the public's confidence in journalism. The Blair scandal forced the *New York Times* to look inwards at a time when its gaze should have been directed elsewhere. In the minds of the Bush administration and the public alike, the scandals confirmed their own beliefs about the media's failings. At a time when they needed their credibility and reputation, the mainstream media was hindered thanks to a series of highly embarrassing incidents of plagiarism and other breaches of the ethics of journalism.

Other aspects of the modern media have also eaten into the ability of journalists to confront government during a crisis. The rise of huge multimedia companies and their desire to create synergies in their media divisions, including the news division, is harming journalism and further increasing public distrust towards the media. The fiasco over the attempts to make a film of Private Jessica Lynch's experiences, despite the many flaws in the story, is a depressing sign that hard news is losing out to the wish to maximize profits and use news events for commercial gain. If this trend continues, there is a risk that news will be folded into entertainment: it is an embrace that it may never escape.

News organizations rely on credibility. If the facts are distorted then there is a danger that news reporting will start a slow, steady slide towards subjectivity and bias. The result will be a growing distrust of the media and an increase in partisan journalism. The late Senator Daniel Patrick

Moynihan once said, "Everyone is entitled to his own opinion, but not his own facts." Moynihan's words beg the question, "what happens in a society where there are no longer agreed facts?"

In many ways this is the supreme question posed by the events of the Iraq war, and it has tremendous implications for journalists and politicians alike. While it can be said that the politicization of facts has been created by decades of bitter partisanship in American politics, the events of the war in Iraq finally created the possibility of a serious breach between reality and its perception as stated by journalists and politicians. The rise of aggressive conservative media organizations has helped in this process, but so-called liberal media organizations have also shown themselves well disposed to enter the fray. In consequence, what is in danger in America is factual news reporting that attempts to place events within their context.

Feeling justified in its decision to go to war, the Bush administration has helped to fuel this environment. From the start of the discussions about war, the Bush administration pursued a media policy that, first, laid the foundation for its future approaches by claiming that the media has no "check and balance role"; it then made a series of inflated claims about Iraq to support the need for war and used the media as a delivery system for this message; finally, it stood by while conservative supporters, both inside and outside the media, helped to sow so much confusion that the American public continues to believe that Iraq had nuclear weapons and supported al Qaeda.

Worryingly, in achieving its aim of going to war the Bush administration has pursued a scorched earth policy. It needs to realize, however, that, in doing so, it is burning the ground beneath its own feet. By degrading journalism and politicizing facts, the executive is losing a center ground, where according to the late Senator Moynihan, the agreed facts can be debated. Such ground is desperately needed for genuine political debate and for good, solid, news reporting. If, as a result of the Bush administration's policies, journalism becomes fragmented, politicians should realize that they also have much to lose. The institutions of politics and media are inextricably bound, and the credibility and reputation of one rests with the other.

What should the media do? To overcome the problems created by the Iraq war, the American media must do two things: first, it should develop a new skepticism towards government. In recent times, this has been set aside in favor of a willingness to give the executive the benefit of the doubt. Second, it must hold on to the key tenets of journalism; it must support editorial independence, and it has to develop better ways of verifying facts and find new methods of making journalism accountable. A failure to do so will mean the news media is participating in its own splintering and possible decline.

This is the process started by the Bush administration's media policy before and during the Iraq war, and it could create a slow burning fire that will eventually overtake both the political and media institutions in the United States, creating a subjective and biased environment where perhaps the biggest, most influential factor, is the public's apathy.

NOTES

INTRODUCTION

1. Sir Arthur Conan Doyle, "Silver Blaze," *The Penguin Complete Sherlock Holmes* (Penguin Books, 1981), p. 347.
2. Ibid., p. 349.
3. "Most Americans Support War with Iraq, Shows Pew/CFR Relations," www.cfr.org (Accessed January 1, 2006).
4. "Poll: 70% believe Saddam, 9/11 Link," *USA Today*, September 6, 2003, www.usatoday.com (Accessed January 1, 2006).
5. "57% of Americans think that Saddam Hussein had Links to Al-Qaeda," mr100percent, everything2.com (Accessed January 1, 2006).
6. "Iraq, 9/11, Al Qaeda and Weapons of Mass Destruction: What the Public Believes Now, According to Latest Harris Poll," www.harrisinteractive.com (Accessed January 1, 2006).

CHAPTER 1: THE ROAD TO AWE

1. Frank Desmond, "McCarthy Charges Reds Hold U.S. Jobs," *Wheeling Intelligencer*, February 10, 1950.
2. Edwin R. Bayley, *Joe McCarthy and the Press* (Wisconsin University Press, 1981), p. 18.
3. Ibid., p. 18.
4. Ibid., p. 20.
5. Ibid., p. 20.
6. Ibid., p. 21.

7. Edwin R. Bayley, *Joe McCarthy and the Press* (Wisconsin University Press, 1981), p. 32.

8. Bayley even gives the example of one newspaper headline that uses the wrong Wisconsin Senator. Edwin R. Bayley, *Joe McCarthy and the Press* (Wisconsin University Press, 1981), p. 18.

9. Ibid., 27.

10. Ibid., 218.

11. "President Delivers State of the Union Speech," The White House, http://www.whitehouse.gov/news/releases (Accessed January 24, 2004).

12. Ibid.

13. Ibid.

14. Ibid.

15. Ibid.

16. Ibid.

17. Walter Pincus, "Bush Faced Dwindling Data on Iraq Nuclear Bid," *Washington Post*, July 16, 2003.

18. Ibid

19. "President's Remarks at the United Nations General Assembly," The White House, http://www.whitehouse.gov/news/releases (Accessed January 27, 2004).

20. Ray Hanania, "Bush Uses Fears, Not Evidence, To Justify Iraq War," *Chicago Daily Herald*, September 13, 2002.

21. John Diamond, "U.S. Assertions Go Beyond Its Intelligence; Questions Raised on Iraq," *USA Today*, September 17, 2002.

22. Ron Hutcheson, "Bush's Speech Offers No Smoking Gun over Iraq," Knight Ridder Washington D.C. Bureau, September 13, 2002.

23. Elisabeth Bumiller, "Traces of Terror: The Strategy; Bush Aides Set Strategy to Sell Policy on Iraq," *New York Times*, September 7, 2002.

24. Scott Lindlaw, "Veep: Saddam Wants Nukes Administration Making Its Case to the Public," *Tallahassee Democrat*, September 9, 2002.

25. Ibid.

26. Elisabeth Bumiller and James Dao, "Cheney Says Peril of a Nuclear Iraq Justifies Attack," *New York Times*, August 26, 2002.

27. Will Lester, "Public Enthusiasm on War with Iraq Lags Behind Political Debate," Associated Press, September 27, 2002.

28. Sonni Efron, "The Nation Across Nation, Critics of Bush Express Support for War," *Los Angeles Times*, September 15, 2002.

29. Rep. Henry A. Waxman, *Iraq on the Record: The Bush Administration's Public Statements on Iraq*, http//www.reform.house.gov/min (accessed February 2, 2005). It should be mentioned that the report was not published at the time that many of the statements were made and does have the considerable benefit of hindsight; nevertheless, the attempt to piece together, through intelligence reports, the comments of experts and news articles, what was actually known

about Iraq's weapons capabilities before the war provides a valuable tool in analyzing the credibility of statements made by Bush administration officials.

30. Rep. Henry A. Waxman, *Iraq on the Record: The Bush Administration's Public Statements on Iraq*, p. 2, http//www.reform.house.gov/min (accessed February 2, 2005). In its methodology section the report states, "For the purposes of the database, a statement is considered 'misleading' if it conflicted with what officials knew at the time or involved the selective use of intelligence or the failure to include essential qualifiers or caveats."

31. Ibid., ii.

32. Ibid., 5.

33. President Bush Outlines Iraqi Threat; Remarks by the President on Iraq, October 7, 2002, http//www.Whitehouse.gov/news (accessed February 4, 2005.)

34. Central Intelligence Agency, Remarks as Prepared for Delivery by Director of Central Intelligence Agency George J. Tenet at Georgetown University (February 5, 2004). Quoted in *Iraq on the Record: The Bush Administration's Public Statements on Iraq*, p. 8, http//www.reform.house .gov/min (accessed February 4, 2005).

CHAPTER 2: WHEN PRESIDENT BITES "WATCHDOG"

1. Dana Milbank, "For Bush, Facts Are Malleable," *Washington Post*, October 22, 2002.

2. Ibid.

3. Mark Halperin, Elizabeth Wilner, and Marc Ambinder, "Teflon Maintenance No Stick Takes Work," ABC News.com, October 22, 2004, www.abcnews.go.co (Accessed August 1, 2005).

4. Ibid.

5. Nicholas Confessore, "Beat the Press," *The American Prospect*, March 11, 2002, www.prospect.org (Accessed August 1, 2005).

6. Pool Reports are summaries of the president's activities meant only for internal use among the White House correspondents.

7. Ken Auletta, "Fortress Bush," *Backstory: Inside the Business of News*, (Penguin (USA) Inc., 2003), p. 323.

8. Harry Jaffe, "Pentagon to *Washington Post* Reporter Ricks: Get Lost," *Online Washingtonian*, December 29, 2003, www.washingtonian.com (Accessed August 2, 2005).

9. E-mail from Jonathan Weisman, March 16, 2003, Poynter Institute, www.poynter.org (Accessed August 2, 2005.)

10. Ibid.

11. Ken Auletta, "Fortress Bush," *Backstory: Inside the Business of News*, (Penguin (USA) Inc., 2003), p. 319.

12. Ibid., p. 319.

13. "Veteran White House Correspondent Helen Thomas on Bush and the State of the Media," *Democracy Now!*, April 8, 2004, www.democracynow.org (Accessed July 31, 2005).

14. Ken Auletta, "Fortress Bush," *Backstory: Inside the Business of News*, (Penguin (USA) Inc., 2003), p. 319.

15. Lori Robertson, "In Control," *American Journalism Review*, February/ March issue, www.ajr.org (Accessed July 31, 2005).

16. Ibid.

17. Jack Shafer, "The Propaganda President," *Slate Magazine*, www.slate. msn.com (Accessed July 31, 2005)

18. Lori Robertson, "In Control," *American Journalism Review*, February/ March issue, www.ajr.org (Accessed July 31, 2005).

19. Eri Boehlert, "Tearing Down the Press," Salon.com news, www. salon.com (Accessed July 31, 2005.).

20. "Is Bush Leapfrogging the National Media or the Truth," Editorial, *Old Speak*, The Rutherford Institute, October 15, 2003, www.Rutherford.org (Accessed July 31, 2005).

21. Edmund Burke was an Irish-born statesman and political thinker.

22. Ken Auletta, "Fortress Bush," *Backstory: Inside the Business of News*, (Penguin (USA) Inc., 2003), p. 308.

23. Ibid., p. 308. It is also interesting to note that Card himself is an unelected official albeit speaking on behalf of an elected official, namely the president!

24. Timothy W. Maier, "The Crumbling of the Fourth Estate," *The Nation*, May 24, 2004.

25. Ibid.

26. Ibid.

27. Oliver Burkeman, "All the News That's Fit to Print—or So We Thought," *The Guardian* (London), May 13, 2003.

28. Ashcroft Memorandum to heads of federal departments and agencies.

29. Bill Berkowitz, "Freedom of Information Act on the Ropes," October 11, 2002, The Freedom of Information Center, www.foi.missouri.edu (Accessed August 6, 2005).

30. Ibid.

31. Timothy W. Maier, "Bush Team Thumbs Its Nose at FOIA," *Insight on the News*, April 29, 2002.

32. Charles Lewis, "Freedom of Information Under Attack," (undated), *Nieman Watchdog*, www.niemanwatchdog.org (Accessed August 7, 2005).

33. Lance Gay, "9/11 Panel Says Too Many Documents Stamped Secret," Scripps Howard News Service, May 14, 2004, The Freedom of Information Center, www.foi.missouri.edu (Accessed August 6, 2005).

34. William Fisher, "Fresh Skirmishes in the Information Wars," March 31, 2005, AntiWar.com, www.antiwar.com (Accessed August 7, 2005).

35. Ibid.

36. Michelle Chen, "Pentagon Seeks Greater Immunity from Freedom of Information Act," *The New Standard*, www.newsstandardnews.net (Accessed August 7, 2005).

37. Ashcroft Memorandum to heads of federal departments and agencies.

38. Michelle Chen, "Pentagon Seeks Greater Immunity from Freedom of Information Act," *The New Standard*, www.newsstandardnews.net (Accessed August 7, 2005).

CHAPTER 3: DISSENT AND PATRIOTISM: THE ARM'S LENGTH PRINCIPLE

1. Bill Maher quoted in Celestine Bohlen, "In the New War on Terrorism, Words are Weapons, Too," *New York Times*, September 29, 2001.

2. "We Love the Liberties They Hate," *New York Times*, September 30, 2001.

3. *New York Times Co. v. Sullivan* 376 US 254 (1964).

4. Norman Solomon, "The Pentagon Papers," *Z magazine*, July/August 2001, www.thirdworldtraveller.com (Accessed December 13, 2004).

5. John W. Johnson, "The Role of a Free Media," Democracy Papers, USINFO.STATE.GOV, www.usinfostate.gov (Accessed August 11, 2005).

6. David Halberstam, *The Powers That Be* (Alfred A. Knopf Inc. 1979), p. 568.

7. Ibid., pp. 568–570.

8. Ibid., p. 573.

9. Ibid., p. 573.

10. "The Pentagon Papers Case," US Info, www.usinfo.state.gov (Accessed April 10, 2006).

11. *New York Times v. United States* [403 U.S. 713].

12. "The Pentagon Papers Case, Issues of Democracy," *USIA Electronic Journal*, Vol. 2, No. 1, February 1997, www.usinfo.state.gov (Accessed August 11, 2005).

13. John Ashcroft, testimony before the Senate Judiciary Committee, December 6, 2001.

14. "You Are Either with Us or Against Us," CNN.com/U.S., November 6, 2001, www.cnn.com (Accessed April 9, 2006).

15. Dana Priest, "Rumsfeld: Criticism at Home, Abroad Encouraging Terrorists," *Washington Post*, September 8, 2003.

16. Ibid.

17. Ibid.

18. "Powell Briefs U.N. on Iraq," *USA Today*, Copyright Associated Press, www.usatoday.com (Accessed August 14, 2005).

19. Dick Meyer, "Polls, Powell and the Iraq Campaign," February 7, 2003, CBS, www.cbsnews.com (Accessed August 14, 2005).

20. "President Bush: Job Ratings," *Newsweek* poll conducted by Princeton Survey Research Associates, summarized on PollingReport.com, www.pollingreport.com

21. Howard Kurtz, "Eason Jordan, Quote, Unquote," *Washington Post*, February 8, 2005.

22. Ibid.

23. Ibid.

24. Howard Kurtz, "CNN's Jordan Resigns Over Iraq Remarks," *Washington Post*, February 12, 2005.

CHAPTER 4: ALL QUIET ON THE HOME FRONT

1. Paul Waldie, "NYSE Shows Al-Jazeera the Door," *Globe and Mail*, March 25, 2003.

2. Alex Wade, "The Untouchables," *Guardian* (London), March 31, 2003.)

3. Ibid.

4. Thomas S. Mulligan, "Nasdaq Joins in Ban of Al Jazeera Stock Market Cites the TV Network's Airing of Images of Dead and Captured U.S. Soldiers," *Los Angeles Times*, March 26, 2003.

5. "Al-Jazeera's Un-embeds," *Financial Times* (United Kingdom), March 26, 2003.

6. Thomas S. Mulligan, "Nasdaq Joins in Ban of Al Jazeera Stock Market Cites the TV Network's Airing of Images of Dead and Captured U.S. Soldiers," *Los Angeles Times*, March 26, 2003.

7. "Al-Jazeera's Correspondents' Credentials Revoked," Press Release, March 25, 2003, Committee to Protect Journalists, www.cpj.org, July 15, 2003.

8. Janet Kolodzy and Wade S. Ricks, "Stocks Are Down and Al-Jazeera's Out," *American Journalism Review*, May 1, 2003.

9. Henry Norr and Amy Goodman, "San Francisco Chronicle Fires Reporter for Attending Peace Protest," *Democracy Now!*, April 24, 2003, www.democracynow.org, August 11, 2003.

10. Ibid.

11. Brandon Moeller and Brent Flynn, "Columnist Silenced After Protesting," Interview, KPFT News, www.kpft.org, July 16, 2003.

12. Jonathan Sidener, "Hackers, Web Hosting Companies become Censors of War Coverage," *San Diego Union-Tribune*, March 28, 2003.

13. Ibid.

14. Kinley Levack, "Censorship in Vogue for Yellowtimes.org," *Econtent*, Vol. 26, No. 6.

15. "Some Critical Voices Face Censorship," FAIR, April 13, 2003, www.fair.org (Accessed April 10, 2006).

16. Mark McGuire, "We don't Need to See Pearl Die," *Times Union* Albany, NY, June 11, 2003.

17. Alisa Solomon, "The Big Chill," *Nation*, June 2, 2003.

18. Ibid.

19. President George W. Bush, Address to a Joint Session of Congress, September 20, 2001.

20. "Behind Pro war Protests, a Company with Ties to Bush," *International Herald Tribune*, March 26, 2003.

21. Tim Jones, "Rally Sponsorship by Clear Channel Raises Questions," *Chicago Tribune*, March 19, 2003.

22. Ibid.

23. Ibid.

24. John Schwartz and Geraldine Fabrikant, "War Puts Radio Giant on the Defensive," *New York Times*, March 31, 2003.

25. Lisa de Moraes, "Producer is a Casualty in CBS's 'Hitler Mini-series,' " *Washington Post*, April 11, 2003.

26. "Bin Laden Joke Steams Sikhs," *New York Post*, p. 6, April 3, 2003.

27. John Podhoretz, "A Hitler Mini-series Meant to Bash Bush," *New York Post*, April 9, 2003.

28. Lisa de Moraes, "Producer is a Casualty in CBS's 'Hitler Mini-series,' " *Washington Post*, April 11, 2003.

29. Joanne Ostrow, "Hollywood Goes Paranoid," *Denver Post*, May 22, 2003.

30. "Americans Want to Impeach the President—the TV version: More than 57,000 Petition Against West Wing Actor Sheen's politics," Ottawa Citizen, Jennifer Campbell, March 5, 2003.

31. "2 NBC Stars in Dueling War Ads," *Milwaukee Journal Sentinel*, Hollywood Reporter, March 1, 2003.

32. Anna Cuenca, "Hollywood Finds Criticizing Iraq War Carries a Hefty Price," Agence France-Presse, April 2, 2003.

33. Renee Graham, "Even Big-Mouthed Celebs Have the Right to Speak Their Minds," *Chicago Tribune*, April 18, 2003.

34. Leonara LaPeter, "Charity Calls off Event with Sarandon," *St. Petersburg Times*, March 27, 2003.

35. "A Chill Wind is Blowing in this Nation," Transcript of Speech given by Actor Tim Robbins at the National Press Club Washington D.C., April 15, 2003, www.commondreams.org, August 14, 2003.

36. "Justice Scalia Says War Warrants Rights Recess," Associated Press, March 19, 2003.

37. "People—Bush: Taking the Diplomatic Effort to the Limit," *The Hotline*, March 14, 2003.

CHAPTER 5: THE PRISON, THE GENERAL, AND THE FLEXIBLE BROADCASTER

1. Kathleen T. Rhem, "Military Commander Details Mission That Killed Hussein's Sons," American Forces Information Service: News Articles,

July 23, 2003, United States Department of Defense, www.defenselink.mil (Accessed August 29, 2005).

2. Paul Cochrane, "To Show or Not to Show?" Worldpress.org, June 10, 2004, www.worldpress.org (Accessed August 29, 2005).

3. Antoine Blua, "Iraq: Grisly Photos of Hussein's Sons Spark Ethical Concerns," Radio Free Europe/Radio Liberty, www.rferl.org (Accessed August 29, 2005).

4. Ibid.

5. "A Grisly Exhibition of Death," *Guardian* (London), July 26, 2003.

6. Antoine Blua, "Iraq: Grisly Photos of Hussein's Sons Spark Ethical Concerns," Radio Free Europe/Radio Liberty, www.rferl.org (Accessed August 29, 2005).

7. Ibid.

8. "Pictures of the Dead Spark Moral Debate, July 25, 2003," SMH.com.au, www.smh.com (Accessed August 29, 2005).

9. David Bauder, "Media Grapples With Hussein Sons Corpse Photos," Associated Press, July 24, 2003.

10. Ibid.

11. "Media Grapples With Hussein Sons Corpse Photos," David Bauder, Associated Press, July 24, 2003.

12. Lawrence M. Hinman, "Hussein Photos Serve to Inform or Inflame?," *San Diego Union-Tribune*, July 25, 2003.

13. "Pictures of Dead Spark Moral Debate, July 25, 2003," SMH.com.au, www.smh.com.au (Accessed August 29, 2005).

14. Sherry Ricchiardi, "Missed Signals," *American Journalism Review*, August/September 2004 Issue, www.ajr.org (Accessed August 29, 2005).

15. Ibid.

16. Seymour M. Hersh, "Torture at Abu Ghraib," *New Yorker*, Issue of 2004–05–10, Posted 2004–04–30.

17. Ibid.

18. Ibid.

19. William Scott Malone, "The General and the Journalists," Navy Seals.com, MediaChannel.org, www.mediachannel.org (Accessed August 29, 2005).

20. Ibid.

21. Ibid.

22. "Did Military Try to Suppress Iraq Prison Photos?," Staff, *Editor and Publisher*, May 7, 2004, www.independent-media.tv (Accessed August 29, 2005).

23. Ibid.

24. Ibid.

25. Ibid.

26. Ibid.

27. David Peterson, "Self-Censorship and Torture," *Counterpunch*, May 4, 2004, www.counterpunch.com (Accessed September 5, 2005).

28. "CBS News Says It Held Iraq Prison Abuse Story," Associated Press, May 4, 2004, www.ctv.ca (Accessed August 29, 2005).

29. Ibid.

30. Sherry Ricchiardi, "Missed Signals," *American Journalism Review*, August/September 2004 Issue, www.ajr.org (Accessed August 29, 2005).

31. Jonah Goldberg, "Media Missteps," May 7, 2004, *National Review Online*, wwwnationalreview.com (Accessed August 29, 2005).

32. Ibid.

33. "CBS News Says It Held Iraqi Prison Abuse Story," Associated Press, May 4, 2005, www.ctv.ca (Accessed August 29, 2005).

34. Christopher Hanson, "Tortured Logic," *Columbia Journalism Review* (Undated).

35. There is an interesting final chapter to the Abu Ghraib case. In late September 2005, in a case brought by the American Civil Liberties Union (ACLU), a U.S. district judge ruled that the American public were entitled to see a further 87 unseen images. The government had previously refused to release the pictures under the FOIA. Before the court, lawyers for the government had argued that the release of the pictures would aid the insurgency. Explicitly rebutting this argument in his 50-page ruling Judge Hellerstein said, "My task is not to defer to our worst fears, but to interpret and apply the law, in this case, the Freedom of Information Act which advances values important to our society, transparency and accountability in government." The judgment was a victory for open government, but it also revealed the lack of independence displayed by CBS. "Abu Ghraib Images 'Must Appear,'" British Broadcasting Corporation, *www.newsvote.bbc.uk* (Accessed September 30, 2005).

CHAPTER 6: CONCENTRATING ON BIAS

1. Jennifer Lee, On Minot, N.D., Radio, A Single Corporate Voice, *New York Times*, March 29, 2003.

2. Ibid.

3. Ibid.

4. Ibid.

5. Ibid.

6. Susan Schmidt and Vernon Loeb, "She Was Fighting to the Death," *Washington Post*, April 3, 2003.

7. John Kampfner, "Saving Private Lynch Story Flawed," BBC News, May 15, 2003, www.newsvote.bbc.co.uk (Accessed October 5, 2005).

8. Ibid.

9. John Kampfner, "Saving Private Lynch Story Flawed," BBC News, May 15, 2003, www.newsvote.bbc.co.uk (Accessed October 5, 2005).

10. "CBS Backs Down on Lynch Movie," BBC News, undated, www.newsvote.bbc.co.uk (Accessed October 5, 2005).

11. "NBC Going Full Speed With Lynch Biopic," *Pittsburgh Post Gazette*, Unnamed, www.global.factiva.com (Accessed September 27, 2005).

12. "Our views: No Ethics, The Pursuit of Pfc. Lynch is Commercialism Not Journalism," Editorial, *Charleston Gazette*, June 17, 2003.

13. Ibid.

14. Lisa de Moraes, "CBS News Defends Its Many Pitches for a Lynch Interview," *Washington Post*, June 18, 2003.

15. Cunningham Brent, "Re-thinking Objectivity," *Columbia Journalism Review*, July 1, 2003.

16. Bob Panzenbeck, "Cronkite Can't Rationalize Liberal Media Bias," *SUNY-Albany*, September 8, 2003.

17. Ted J. Smith III, "The Media Elite Revisited," *Look Smart*, www.findarticles.com (Accessed October 12, 2005).

18. Ibid.

19. Scott Collins, *Crazy Like a Fox: The Inside Story of How Fox News Beat CNN*, (Penguin Group, 2004), page 78.

20. Ibid.

21. An example of this may be seen in O'Reilly's airing of doubts regarding President Bush's nomination of Harriet Miers to the Supreme Court.

22. www.nydailynews.com/entertainment/story/5153p-48314c.html

23. Jay Rosen, "The Fox News Daily Memo: Is the Fix In?," *Press Think*, October 30, 2003, www.journalism.nyu.edu (Accessed October 26, 2005).

24. "The Fox News Memo," *Poynter Online*, www.poynter.org (Accessed October 26, 2005).

25. Ibid.

26. Harold Meyerson, "Fact-Free News," *Washington Post*, October 15, 2003, www.washingtonpost.com (Accessed October 26, 2005).

27. Timothy Noah, "Fox News Admits Bias," *Slate* magazine, www.slate.msn.com (Accessed October 26, 2005).

28. Ibid.

CHAPTER 7: MEA PULPA

1. Michael R. Gordon and Judith Miller, "Threats and Responses: The Iraqis, U.S. Says Hussein Intensifies Quest for A-Bomb Parts," *New York Times*, September 8, 2002.

2. Ibid.

3. Ibid.

4. James C. Moore, "Not Fit to Print," May 27, 2004, *Salon*, www.salon.com (Accessed October 27, 2005).

5. Ibid.

6. Judith Miller, "Illicit Arms Kept Till Eve of War, Iraqi Scientist Is Said to Assert," *New York Times*, April 21, 2003.

7. James C. Moore, "Not Fit to Print," May 27, 2004, *Salon*, www.salon.com (Accessed October 27, 2005).

8. Rick Mercier, "Viewpoints: Elite Print Media Failed Its Readers on the Iraq war," *The Free Lance-Star*, March 30, 2004.

9. "The Times and Iraq," From the Editors, *New York Times*, May 26, 2004.

10. Ibid.

11. Ibid.

12. Ibid.

13. Daniel Okrent, "Weapons of Mass Destruction? Or Mass Distraction," Public Editor, *New York Times*, May 30, 2004.

14. Ibid.

15. Grant McCool, "NY Times Says It Fell for Iraq Misinformation," Reuters News, May 26, 2004.

16. "Interview: Robert Steele discusses the *New York Times'* admission of shortcomings in some of its Iraqi coverage," NPR: Talk of the Nation, May 26, 2004.

17. Ibid.

18. Jack Shafer, "The Times Scoop That Melted," *Slate* magazine, July 25, 2003, www.slate.com (Accessed November 3, 2005).

19. Jack Shafer, "The Exorcism of the New York Times," *Slate* magazine, October 25, 2005, www.slate.com (Accessed November 3, 2005).

20. Ibid.

21. Peter Johnson, "N.Y. Times Criticized for Quiet Mea Culpa," *USA Today*, www.usatoday.com (Accessed October 28, 2005).

22. Ibid.

23. "Leading US Daily Admits Underplaying Stories Critical of White House Push for Iraq War," Agence France Presse, August 12, 2004, Common Dreams News Center, www.commondreams.org (Accessed October 28, 2004).

24. Ibid.

25. See *Bush at War* and *Plan of Attack*, both by Bob Woodward and published by Simon and Schuster.

26. "Leading US Daily Admits Underplaying Stories Critical of White House Push for Iraq War," Agence France Presse, August 12, 2004, Common Dreams News Center, www.commondreams.org (Accessed October 28, 2004).

27. Howard Kurtz, "The Post on WMDs: An Inside Story," *Washington Post*, August 12, 2004.

28. Ibid.

29. Ibid.

30. Howard Kurtz, "The Post on WMDs: An Inside Story," *Washington Post*, August 12, 2004.

31. Ibid.

32. Howard Kurtz, "New Republic Editors 'Regret' Their Support of Iraq War," *Washington Post*, June 19, 2004.

33. Ibid.

34. Kate Willtrout, "Stahl of *60 Minutes* Says She Regrets Iraq WMD stories," *Virginian-Pilot*, April 22, 2004.

35. Ibid.

36. "Newsman Rather Tells Americans Ask More Questions," Reuters News Service, May 16, 2002.

37. Oscar Wilde, *The Importance of Being Earnest*, 1895, Act I.

38. "The Times and Iraq," From the Editors, The *New York Times*, May 26, 2004 and Howard Kurtz, "The Post on WMDs: An Inside Story," *Washington Post*, August 12, 2004.

CHAPTER 8: REINTRODUCING THE SKEPTIC'S TEST

1. Eric Alterman, "Think Again: The Media and the War: Any Lessons Learned?" October 14, 2005, Center for American Progress, www.americanprogress.org (Accessed November 8, 2005).

2. Ibid.

3. Jonathan Keats, "We Still Have Him to Kick Around, After All; Nixon's Efforts to Control the Press Gave Birth to Modern Media Skepticism," *Christian Science Monitor*, October 9, 2003.

4. Heather Holiday, "Panel Debate on the Media and Iraq War Raises More Questions than Answers," This Week @UCSD, December 6, 2004, www.ucsdnews.ucsd.edu/thisweek (Accessed November 8, 2005).

5. Ibid.

6. Dan Froomkin, "What's a Press Corps to Do?" *Washington Post*, March 18, 2005, www.washingtonpost.com (Accessed November 11, 2005).

7. Ibid.

8. Ibid.

9. Liz Halloran, "Hiding Behind Anonymity 'Background Briefings' Increase Under Bush, *The Hartford Courant*, September 24, 2004.

10. Ibid.

11. Ibid.

12. Ibid.

13. Jay Rosen, "Stop Us Before We're Briefed Again," *Pressthink*, www.journalism.nyu.edu (Accessed November 8, 2005).

14. Ibid.

15. Ryan Pitts, "APME National Credibility Roundtables Project," *Spokane Spokesman-Review*, June 17, 2005, www.apme-credibility.org (Accessed November 8, 2005).

16. Ibid.

17. Daniel Okrent, "Weapons of Mass Destruction? Or Mass Distraction?" *New York Times*, May 30, 2005.

18. "Confidential News Sources," February 25, 2004, *New York Times* Company, www.nytco.com (Accessed November 8, 2005).

19. Ibid.

20. Ibid.

21. Jack Shafer, "Washington Confidential," *Slate* magazine, www.slate.com (Accessed November 8, 2005).

22. Michael Getler, "A Parting Thought on Iraq Again," *Washington Post*, October 9, 2005, www.washingtonpost.com (Accessed November 8, 2005).

23. Jack Shafer, "Washington Confidential," *Slate* magazine, www.slate.com (Accessed November 8, 2005).

24. "A Failure of Skepticism in Powell Coverage," Fairness & Accuracy in Reporting, February 10, 2003, www.fair.org (Accessed November 11, 2003).

25. Ibid.

26. Ibid.

27. Ibid.

28. "Developing Methods of Verification," Journalism.Org website for the Project for Excellence in Journalism, Journalism.org, www.journalism.org (Accessed November 20, 2005).

29. Jeffrey A. Dvorkin, "BBC Reports: Sentence First. Verdict Afterwards," National Public Radio, February 4, 2004, www.npr.org (Accessed November 8, 2005).

30. Bob Steele, "Editors and Reporters: What They Owe Each Other," Poynter Online, www.poynter.org (Accessed November 8, 2005).

31. Ibid.

32. Eric Alterman, "Think Again: The Media and the War: Any Lessons Learned?" October 14, 2005, Center for American Progress, www.americanprogress.org (Accessed November 8, 2005).

33. Ibid.

BIBLIOGRAPHY

BY TITLE

"2 NBC Stars in Dueling War Ads," *Milwaukee Journal Sentinel*, Hollywood Reporter, March 1, 2003.

"57% of Americans Think that Saddam Hussein Had Links to Al-Qaeda (idea)," mr100percent, www.everything2.com [January 1, 2006].

"A Failure of Skepticism in Powell Coverage, Disproof of previous claims underlines Need for Scrutiny," FAIR, February 10, 200, www.fair.org [November 11, 2005].

"A Grisly Exhibition of Death," *Guardian*, July 26, 2003.

"Abu Ghraib," www.rotten.com [August 29, 2005].

"Abuse of Iraqi POWs By GIs Probed," CBS News, www.cbsnews.com, April 28, 2004 [August 29, 2005].

"Accusation of Iraqi Ties With Al-Qaeda Very Shaky," Opinion, *Palm Beach Post*, February 13, 2003.

"Al-Jazeera's Un-embeds," *The Financial Times* (United Kingdom), March 26, 2003.

"AP Reminds Staff about Policy," Associated Press, November 8, 2005.

"Baradei—UN Inspectors did not Find Prohibited Nuclear Activities in Iraq," Middle East News Agency, January 27, 2003.

"Behind Pro War Protests, a Company with Ties to Bush," *International Herald Tribune*, March 26, 2003.

"Bin Laden Joke Steams Sikhs," *The New York Post*, P. 6, April 3, 2003.

"Bush: Don't Wait for Mushroom Cloud," CNN.com, www.cnn.com [January 5, 2001].

"Bush Media Challenges Recall Those of JFK," *Penn State News*, April 5, 2004, www.psu.edu/ur [September 8, 2005].

"Bush to Press: 'Your're Assuming That You Represent the Public. I Don't Accept That.' " *Pressthink*, April 25, 2004, www.journalism.nyu.edu [July 31, 2005].

"Bush: War not Inciting Terrorists," CNN.com, www.cnn.com [December 7, 2004].

"Call to Action over Nukes," *Herald-Sun*, September 10, 2002.

"Case Study: Jack Kelley and *USA Today*," Online News Hour, www.pbs.org [January 24, 2006].

"CBS Backs Down on Lynch Movie," BBC News, www.newsvote.bbc.co.uk [September 20, 2005].

"CBS Fires Four after Its Report is Released on National Guard Story," Associated Press.

"CBS News Says It Held Iraq Prison Abuse Story," Associated Press, May 4, 2004.

"CBS Sat on Prisoner Abuse/torture Story for Almost Two Weeks," May 4, 2004, www.chrisshumway.tripod.com [August 29, 2005].

"Cheney Says No Decision on *US* Strike Against Iraq," Reuters News, March 19, 2002.

"Developing Methods of Verification," Journalism.org, www.journalism.org [November 20, 2005].

"Did Military Try to Suppress Iraq Prison Photos, *Editor & Publisher*, May 7, 2004, www.editorandpublisher.com [August 29, 2005].

"Don't Answer Questions for Me, Bush Tells Musharraf," Press Trust of India, December 4, 2004.

"Ex-editor slams N.Y. Times over Iraq Stories Note/Defends Reporting on WMDs That Paper Now Says Was Rushed," *Houston Chronicle*, May 28, 2004.

"Five Times More Journalists Are Liberal Than Conservative," CyberAlert, www.mrc.org [January 25, 2006].

"Four Corners: Spinning the Tubes—Timeline," ABC Online, www.abc.net.au [April 25, 2005].

"How They Voted//United States Congress," *Springfield Union-News*, October 13, 2002.

"The Hutton Inquiry and its Impact," The *Guardian*, February 6, 2004.

"Interview: Robert Steele discusses The New York Times' admission of shortcomings in some of its Iraq coverage," NPR: Talk of the Nation, May 26, 2004.

"Iraq, 9/11, Al-Qaeda and Weapons of Mass Destruction: What the Public Believes Now, According to Latest Harris Poll," Harris Interactive, www.harrisinteractive.com [January 1, 2006].

"Iraq, Abu Ghraib Prison, And Media Treason," May 3, 2004, www.aether.com [August 29, 2005].

"Iraq on the Record," Prepared for Rep. Henry A. Waxman, www.reform. house.go/min [February 2, 2005].

"Iraqi WMDs," www.rotten.com [November 30, 2004].

"Is Bush Leapfrogging the National Media or the Truth," oldSpeak, October 15, 2003, www.rutherford.org [July 4, 2005].

"Journalists Face Jail Time," Opinion, The *New York Times*, August 11, 2004.

"Justice Scalia Says War Warrants Rights Recess," Associated Press, March 19, 2003.

"Leading US Daily Admits Underplaying Stories Critical of White House Push for Iraq War," Agence France Presse, August 12, 2004.

"Minnesotans Owe You an Apology," Captain's Quarters, May 7, 2004, www. captain'squartersblog.com [August 29, 2005].

"The Myth of the Media's Role in Vietnam," Fairness and Accuracy in Reporting (FAIR), www.fair.org [August 29, 2005].

"The Nation; Interview With President Bush/The Transcript; 'I'm a War President,' Bush Says," From Reuters, *Los Angeles Times*, February 9, 2004.

"NBC Going Full Speed With Lynch Biopic," *Pittsburg Post-Gazette*, April 15, 2003.

"New York Times Apologises for Flawed Reporting," *The Age*, May 27, 2004, www.theage.com.au [October 28, 2005].

"Now They Tell Us: An Exchange," February 26, 2004, www.williambowles.info [August 23, 2004].

"NY Times Says It Was Misinformed by Iraqi Exiles," Reuters News, May 26, 2004.

"Our views: No ethics, The pursuit of Pfc. Lynch is Commercialism, not Journalism," *Charleston Gazette*, June 17, 2003.

"The Pentagon Papers and Their Continuing Significance," History of the Pentagon Papers, www.vva.org [August 11, 2005].

"The Pentagon Papers Case," Issues of Democracy, *USIA Electronic Journal*, Vol. 2, No.1, February 1997, www.usinfo.state.gov [August 11, 2005].

"The Pentagon Papers: Secrets and Lies and Audiotapes," The National Security Archive, www2gwu.edu [December 13, 2004].

"Pentagon to Washington Post Reporter Ricks: Get Lost," *Online Washingtonian*, www.Washingtonian.com [August 2, 2005].

"People—Bush: Taking the Diplomatic Effort to the Limit," *The Hotline*, March 14, 2003.

"Poll: 70% believe Saddam, 9–11 link," *USA Today*, www.usatoday.com [January 1, 2006].

"Polls, Powell and the Iraq Campaign," CBS News, February 7, 2003, www.cbsnews.com [August 14, 2005].

"Powell Briefs U.N. on Iraq," Associated Press, USA Today.com, www.usatoday.com [August 14, 2005].

"Powell: Tape Shows bin Laden 'in Partnership With Iraq,' " NewMax.com, www.newsmax.com [December 6, 2004].

"President, House Leadership Agree on Iraq Resolution," The White House, October 2, 2002, www.whitehouse.gov (Accessed April 10, 2006)

"Prior Restraints and the Presumption of Unconstitutionality," www.law.umkc.edu [December 13, 2004].

"Proof That the *Washington Post* and the White House Press Corps Wear Knee Pads: Breathe Deeply and Swallow," Buzzflash News Analysis, Poynter Online, www.poynter.org [November 28, 2005].

"Release of Photos of Bodies Raises Ethics Concerns," CNN.com, www.cnn.com [August 29, 2005].

"Right-Wing: When in Doubt, Attack People's Patriotism," Center for American Progress, www.americanprogress.org [August 14, 2005].

"Should the Media Investigate Errors In Its Coverage leading Up to the Invasion of Iraq," *Democracy Now!*, February 11, 2004, www.democracynow,org [July 31, 2005].

"Sulzberger Dodged the Question," *Editor & Publisher*, March 25, 2004, www. editorandpublisher.com [March 30, 2004].

"The *Times* and Iraq," The *New York Times*, May 26, 2004.

"The *Times* and Iraq: A Sample of Coverage," From the Editors, The *New York Times*, www.nytimes.com [May 27, 2004].

"Top Bush Officials Push Case Against Saddam," CNN.com, September 8, 2002, www.cnn.com [January 26, 2005].

"US Says Germany 'in denial' over Possible bin Laden Tape," Agence France-Presse, February 12, 2003.

"US Warns of al-Qaeda/Iraq 'Nightmare,'" NewsMax.com, www.newsmax.-com [December 12, 2004].

"Veteran White House Correspondent Helen Thomas On Bush and the State of the Media," *Democracy Now!*, April 8, 2004, www.democracynow.org [July 31, 2005].

"Weapons-Grade Plutonium Possibly Found at Iraqi Nuke Complex," Fox News, April 11, 2003, www.foxnews.com [August 25, 2004].

"Weapons of Mass Destruction: Who Said What When," *Counterpunch*, www.counterpunch.org [April 28, 2004].

BY AUTHOR

Ackerman, Seth, "The Most Biased Name in News," *Extra!*, August 2001, www.fair.org [December 7, 2004].

Adelman, Ken, "Saddam's State of Terror," *Wall Street Journal*, August 28, 2002.

Alterman, Eric, "Bush's War on the Press," *Nation*, May 9, 2005.

Alterman, Eric, "Think Again: The Media and the War: Any Lessons Learned," October 14, 2005, www.americanprogress.org [November 8, 2005].

Anderson, Kevin, "How Free is American Information," BBC News, www. newsvote.bbc.co.uk [August 6, 2005].

Auletta, Ken, *Backstory: Inside the Business of News*, Penguin Press, New York, 2003.

Baker, Russ, " 'Scoops' and Truth at the Times," *Nation*, June 23, 2003, www.thenation.com [October 28, 2003].

Bandler, James, "Paper Trial: *New York Times* Finds Its Watchdog Has a Strong Bite," *Wall Street Journal*, July 12, 2004.

Barstow, David William J. Broad, and Jeff Gerth, "The Nuclear Card: The Aluminium Tube Story—A Special Report," *New York Times*, October 3, 2004.

Bauder, David, "CBS News Says It Held Off on Prisoner Abuse Story for Two Weeks," Associated Press, May 3, 2004.

Bauder, David, "Media Grapples With Hussein Son's Corpse Photos," July 24, 2003, Associated Press.

Bennett, Phil, "*Washington Post* Editor Comments on Survey," Associated Press, April 4, 2005.

Berkowitz, Bill, "Freedom of Information Act on the Ropes," The Freedom of Information Center, October 11, 2002, www.foi.missouri.edu [August 6, 2005].

Berman, Ari, "Polls Suggest Media Failure in Pre-War Coverage," *Editor & Publisher*, www.editorandpublisher.com [January 24, 2006].

Blair, David and Toby Harnden, "US to Show 'Gruesome' Pictures of Saddam Sons," *Daily Telegraph* (London) July 24, 2003.

Blua, Antonia, "Iraq: Grisly Photos of Hussein's Sons Spark Ethical Concerns," Radio Free Europe/Radio Liberty, www.rferl.or [August 29, 2005].

Boehlert, Eric, "Tearing Down the Press," *Salon*, March 2, 2005, www.salon.com [November 28, 2005].

Bredemeier, Mark, "Conservative Views Sneaking into Liberal Media," *The Kansas City Star*, November 15, 2003.

Bumiller, Elisabeth and James Dao, "Cheney Says Peril of a Nuclear Iraq Justifies an Attack," *The New York Times*, August 27, 2002.

Bush, Jr., George W., President, Address to a Joint Session of Congress, September 20, 2001.

Butler, Amir, "Patriotism: Defending the Indefensible," www.atrueword.com [August 14, 2005].

Byrne, Dennis, "Can the News Media Cover Bush Fairly?" *Chicago Tribune*, November 10, 2003.

Campbell, Jennifer, "Americans Want to Impeach the President—the TV version: More than 57,000 petition against West Wing actor Sheen's politics," *Ottawa Citizen*, March 5, 2003.

Chen, Michelle, "Perntagon Seeks Greater Immunity from Freedom of Information Act," *The News Standard*, www.newstandard.net [August 7, 2005].

Cienski, Jan, "Bush Presses Forward Where Father Pulled back: Special Report: How It Came to This: The Unfinished War," *National Post*, March 15, 2003.

Cloud, David S., "Bush Efforts to Tie Saddam to al Qaeda Lack Proof," *Wall Street Journal*, October 23, 2002.

Cochrane, Paul, "To Show or Not to Show? Worldpress.org, June 10, 2004, www.worldpress.org [August 29, 2005].

Cohen, Jeff, "Propaganda from the Middle of the Road," *Extra!*, October/ November 1989, www.fair.org [September 27, 2005].

Cohen, William S., "The Real Case Against Iraq," *Wall Street Journal*, February 5, 2003.

Collins, Scott, *Crazy Like a Fox: The Inside Story of How Fox News Beat CNN*, Penguin Press, New York, 2004.

Committee to Protect Journalists, "Al-Jazeera's Correspondents' Credentials Revoked, Press Release, March 25, 2003, www.cpj.org, July 15, 2003.

Confessore, Nicholas, "Beat the Press: Does the White House Have a Blacklist," *The American Prospect*, www.prospect.org [August 2, 2005].

Corn, David, "George Won't be Reading This," *LA Weekly*, October 31, 2003, www.laweekly.com [January 25, 2006].

Crary, David, "Survey Shows Many Newspapers Permit Use of Anonymous Sources," Associated Press, November 8, 2005.

Crumley, Bruce, "Doubting Iraq's Ties to al-Qaeda," *Time Magazine*, March 3, 2003.

Cuenca, Anna, "Hollywood Finds Criticizing Iraq War Carries a Hefty Price," Agence France-Presse, April 2, 2003.

Cunningham, Brent, "Re-thinking Objectivity," *Columbia Journalism Review*, July 1, 2003.

Dalglish, Lucy, "Severe Threat to Freedom of Information," mediachannel.org, September 15, 2004, [January 24, 2006].

"Dana Milbank on Covering the White House and Nicknames We Can't Publish," *CJR Daily*, February 20, 2004, www.cjrdaily.org [December 13, 2004].

Defensor, Benjamin G., "What is Media Doing to Journalism?" *BusinessWorld*, September 2, 2004.

Dotinga, Randy, "Unnamed Sources: Essential or Overused?" *Christian Science Monitor*, August 12, 2004.

Dowd, Maureen, "Woman of Mass Destruction," *New York Times*, October 22, 2005.

Dvorkin, Jeffrey A., "BBC Reports: Sentence first, Verdict Afterwards?" National Public Radio, February 4, 2004, www.npr.org [November 8, 2005].

Edwards, David, "Iraq and Nuclear Weapons," *Z magazine*, September 5, 2002, www.zmag.org [August 25, 2004].

Efron, Sonni, "The Nation Across Nation, Critics of Bush Express Support for Iraq War," *Los Angeles Times*, September 15, 2002.

Elliott, Michael, "Countdown to War," *Time Magazine*, February 17, 2003.

Feinstein, Lee, "Most Americans Support War with Iraq, Shows New Pew/CFR Poll— Commentary by Lee Feinstein," Council on Foreign Relations, www.cfr.org [January 1, 2006].

Ferraro, Thomas, "US Cites New Evidence Saddam Seeking Nuclear Bomb," Reuters News, September 9, 2002.

Fisher, William, "Fresh Skirmishes in the Information Wars," AntiWar.com, www.antiwar.com, [August 7, 2005].

Fishgold, Martin and David Swanson, "Censorship Adds to Outrage Over Torture," www.opednews.com [August 29, 2005].

Fishgold, Martin and David Swanson, "Censorship Adds to Outrage Over Torture," OpEdNews.com, wwwopednews.com [January 25, 2006].

Fleischer, Ari, Press Briefing, December 2, 2002, www.whitehouse.gov [November 30, 2004].

Folkenflik, David, "Iraq Prison Story Tough to Hold Off On, CBS Says," baltimoresun.com, May 5, 2004, www.baltimoresun.com [August 29, 2005].

Four Corners, Timeline, ABC Online, www.abc.net.au [July 4, 2005].

Fricker, Mary and Erin Allday, "Critics Say Rule Change Will Mean Fewer Voices in Media," *Press Democrat*, June 9, 2003.

Fritz, Ben, Bryan Keefer, and Brendan Nyhan, *All the President's Spin*, Simon and Schuster, New York, 2004.

Froomkin, Dan, "Battle Over Background Briefings," The *Washington Post*, May 4, 2004.

Froomkin, Dan, "What's A Press Corps to Do?" The *Washington Post*, March 18, 2005.

Gay, Lance, "9/11 Panel Says too Many Documents Stamped Secret," Scripps Howard News Service, May 14, 2004, www.foi.missouri.edu [August 7, 2005].

Gellman, Barton and Walter Pincus, "Depiction of Threat Outgrew Supporting Evidence," *The Washington Post*, August 10, 2003.

Getler, Michael, "Looking Back Before the War," The *Washington Post*, June 20, 2004.

Getler, Michael, "A Parting Though on Iraq, Again," *The Washington Post*, October 9, 2005.

Goldberg, Jonah, "Uneven Standard," *National Review Online*, May 12, 2004, www.nationalreview.com [August 29, 2005].

Goldberg, Jonah, "Media Missteps," *National Review Online*, May 7, 2005, www.nationalreview.com [August 29, 2005].

Gordon, Michael R. and Judith Miller, "U.S. Says Hussein Intensifies Quest for A-Bomb Parts," The *New York Times*, September 8, 2002.

Graham, Renee, (*The Boston Globe*), "Even Big-Mouthed Celebs Have the Right to Speak Their Minds," *Chicago Tribune*, April 18, 2003.

Greenberg, David, "The Watergate Papers," *Slate Magazine*, February 9, 2005, www.slate.com [February 11, 2005].

Gutierrez, Miren, "Fewer Players, Less Freedom," Inter-Press Service, March 20, 2004.

Halberstam, David, *The Powers That Be*, Alfred A. Knopf, Inc., New York, 1979.

Halloran, Liz, "Hiding Behind Anonymity 'Background Briefings' Increase Under Bush," *The Hartford Courant*, September 24, 2004.

Hann, Michael, "What the US Papers Don't Say," *Guardian*, April 30, 2004.

Hanson, Christopher, "Tortured Logic," *Columbia Journalism Review*, July/August 2004 [August 29, 2005].

Haven, Paul, "An al-Qaeda Link to Iraq Would be Unusual, Scary," *Philadelphia Inquirer*, January 30, 2003.

Holiday, Heather, "Panel Debate on the Media and Iraq War Raises More Questions Than Answers," December 6, 2004, www.ucsd.edu [November 8, 2005].

Hutcheson, Ron, "Bush Speech Offers No Smoking Guns over Iraq," Knight-Ridder Tribune News, September 13, 2002.

Interview with Vice-President Dick Cheney, NBC, *"Meet the Press,"* [Transcript] March 16, 2003.

Jackson Jr., William E., "Real 'NY Times Scandal: Hyping WMDs in Iraq," *Editor & Publisher*, June 17, 2003, www.editorandpublisher.com [January 25, 2006].

Jehl, Douglas, "Stung by Exiles' Role, CIA Orders Changes," *International Herald Tribune*, February 14, 2004.

Jehl, Douglas and David E. Sanger, "Powell Presses C.I.A. on Faulty Intelligence on Iraq Arms," *New York Times*, June 2, 2004.

Jensen, Robert, "News Media Industry's Criticism of Iraq Coverage Reveals Deeper Problems With Mainstream Journalists' Conception of News," Common Dreams News Center, www.commondreams.org [December 6, 2004].

Jimenez, Marina, "61% of Muslims Say Arabs not behind Sept. 11: Poll: 77% Say War not Justified," *National Post*, February 28, 2002.

Johnson, Peter, *"N.Y. Times'* Criticized for Quiet Mea Culpa," *USA Today*, May 27, 2004.

Jones, Chris, "Access is Casualty of War," Sidelines Online, www.mtsusidelines.com [February 5, 2004]

Jones, Tim, "Rally Sponsorship by Clear Channel Raises Questions," *Chicago Tribune*, March 19, 2003.

Kane, Eugene, "Truth Was a Key Casualty in Jessica Lynch Rescue Tale," *Milwaukee Journal Sentinel*, June 1, 2003.

Keats, Jonathan, "We Still Have Him to Kick Around, after all; Nixon's Efforts to Control the Press Gave Birth to Modern Media Scepticism," *Christian Science Monitor*, October 9, 2003.

Kinsley, Michael, "Filter Tips," *Slate Magazine*, October 16, 2003, www.slate.msn.com [July 31, 2005].

Kolodzy, Janet and Ricks, Wade S., "Stocks Are Down and Al-Jazeera's Out," and *American Journalism Review*, May 1, 2003.

Korb, Lawrence J. and John Halpin, "Cover-Up of Abu Ghraib Torture Puts Troops at Risk," May 11, 2004, www.americanprogress.org [August 29, 2005].

Krugman, Paul, "Dead Parrot Society," *New York Times*, October 25, 2002.

Kurtz, Howard, "Rick Bragg Quits At *New York Times*," *Washington Post*, May 29, 2003.

Kurtz, Howard, "New Republic Editors 'Regret' Their Support of Iraq War," *Washington Post*, June 19, 2004.

Kurtz, Howard, "The Post on WMDs: An Inside Story," *Washington Post*, August 12, 2004.

Kurtz, Howard, "Writer Backing Bush Plan Had Gotten Federal Contract," *Washington Post*, January 26, 2005.

Kurtz, Howard, "CNN's Jordan Resigns Over Iraq Remarks," *Washington Post*, February 12, 2005.

Landay, Jonathan S. and Tish Wells, "Iraqi Exiles Give False Information to Media," Herald.com, March 16, 2004, www.miami.com [May 27, 2004].

LaPeter, Leonara, "Charity Calls off Event with Sarandon," *St. Petersburg Times*, March 27, 2003.

Larson, Virgil, "Mergers Spawn Critics, Fans," *Omaha World-Herald*, July 12, 2003.

Lee, Jennifer, "On Minot, N.D., Radio, a Single Corporate Voice, *New York Times*, March 29, 2003.

Levack, Kinley, "Censorship in Vogue for Yellowtimes.org," *Econtent*, Volume 26, No. 6.

Lewis, Charles, "Clamping Down on Freedom of the Press," November 22, 2004, The Center for Public Integrity, www.publicintegrity.org [August 29, 2005].

Lewis, Charles, "Freedom of Information Under Attack," Nieman Watchdog, www.niemanwatchdog.org [August 8, 2005].

Lindlaw, Scott, "Veep: Saddam Wants Nukes, Administration Making Its Case to the Public," *Tallahassee Democrat*, September 9, 2002.

Lippmann, Walter, *Public Opinion*, Transaction Publishers, New Jersey, 1991.

Loth, Renee, "Focus on Freedom of Information," *Boston Globe*, September 29, 2004, www.suherald.com [November 25, 2004].

Madigan, Charles M., "Do Americans Really Believe in Free Speech," *Chicago Tribune*, July 4, 2004.

Maier, Timothy W., "The Crumbling of the Fourth Estate," *Insight Magazine*, May 24, 2004.

Maier, Timothy W., "Bush Team Thumbs Its Nose at FOIA," *Insight Magazine*, www.insightmag.com [August 6, 2005].

Malone, William Scott, "The General and the Journalists," www.mediachannel.org [January 25, 2006].

Malwitz, Rick, "Facing Left from the Right, the Media Look Mighty One-sided," *Home News Tribune*, December 7, 2003.

Manjoo, Farhad, "Identity Crisis," *Salon*, May 13, 2005, www.salon.com [May 17, 2005].

Massing, Michael, *Now They Tell Us*, New York Review of Books, New York, 2004.

Massing, Michael, "Unfit to Print," *The New York Review of Books*, Vol. 51, No. 11, June 24, 2004.

Mayer, Jeremy D., "The Contemporary Presidency: The Presidency and Image Management: Discipline in Pursuit of Illusion," *Presidential Studies Quarterly*, Vol. 34, No. 3, September 1, 2004.

Mazzetti, Mark, "PR Meets Psy-Ops in War on Terror," *Los Angeles Times*, December 1, 2004.

McChesney, Robert M., *Corporate Media and the Threat to Democracy*, Seven Stories Press, Canada, 1997.

McChesney, Robert and John Bellamy Foster, "The 'Left-Wing' Media?" *Monthly Review*, Vol. 55, No. 2, June 1, 2003.

McCool, Grant, "NY Times Says It Fell for Iraq Misinformation," Reuters News, May 26, 2004.

McGovern, Ray, "Iraq Posed an Unclear and Dubious Danger," AntiWar.com, June 17, 2003, www.antiwar.com [January 13, 2005].

McGuire, Mark, "We don't Need to See Pearl Die," *Times Union Albany, NY*, June 11, 2003.

McManus, Doyle, "Policy on Iraq: The Times Poll," *Los Angeles Times*, September 2, 2002.

Meckler, Laura, "Reporters Fear Secret-source Principle under Attack," *Milwaukee Journal Sentinel*, August 29, 2004.

Melman, Yossi, "Iraq's Ties to Terror: The Threat Isn't Easy to Read," *New York Times*, February 9, 2003.

Mercier, Rick, "Why the Media Owe You an Apology on Iraq," Common Dreams News Center, www.commondreams.org [December 6, 2004].

Mercier, Rick, "Viewpoints: Elite Print Media Failed Its Readers on the Iraq War," March 30, 2004, www.fredericksburg.com [November 6, 2005].

Milbank, Dana, "For Bush, Facts Are Malleable," *Washington Post*, October 22, 2002.

Milbank, Dana, "Tying Kerry to Terror Tests Rhetorical Limits," *Washington Post*, September 24, 2004.

Milbank, Dana, "My Bias for Mainstream News," The *Washington Post*, March 20, 2005.

Milbank, Dana and Walter Pincus, "White House: CIA Questioned State of the Union Address," The *Washington Post*, July 23, 2003.

Miller, David, "In and Out of the Mainstream," www.medialens.org [October 28, 2005].

Miller, David, (ed.), *Tell Me Lies: Propaganda and Media Distortion in the Attack on Iraq*, Pluto Press, London, 2004.

Miller, Greg and Bob Drogin, "The World Showdown With Iraq," *Los Angeles Times*, January 30, 2003.

Mitchell, Greg, "Public Remains Poorly Informed On Reasons for War," *Editor & Publisher*, August 26, 2004, www.editorandpublisher.com [January 25, 2006].

Moeller, Brandon and Brent Flynn, "Columnist Silenced After Protesting," [Interview], KPFT News, www.kpft.org, July 16, 2003.

Moeller, Susanne D., "Media Coverage of Weapons of Mass Destruction," March 9, 2004, www.64.233.183.104 [February 2, 2005].

Monbiot, George, "Greasing up to power," *Guardian*, July 13, 2004.

Monbiot, George, "Holding the Press to Account for Falsehood," *Guardian*, July 20, 2004.

Monbiot, George, "A Televisual Fairyland," *Guardian*, January 18, 2005.

Mooney, Chris, "Did Our Leading Newspapers Set Too Low a Bar for a Preemptive Attack?" *Columbia Journalism Review*, www.cjr.org [March 4, 2004].

Moore, James C., "Not Fit to Print," Salon, May 27, 2004, www.salon.com [November 7, 2005].

Moraes, Lisa de, "Producer is a Casualty in CBS's 'Hitler Mini-series,'" *Washington Post*, April 11, 2003.

Moraes, Lisa de, "CBS News Defends Its Many Pitches for a Lynch Interview," *Washington Post*, June 18, 2003.

Mosey, Roger, "The BBC Was No Cheerleader for War," *Guardian*, July 27, 2004.

Mostert, Mary, "Is George Bush Unfairly Competing with the Big 5 Media Conglomerates?" www.renewamerica.us [December 7, 2004].

Moyers, Bill, "A Democracy Can Die of Too Many Lies," *Salon*, May 17, 2005, www.salon.com [May 17, 2005].

Moyers, Bill, "Media Concentration Threatens Freedom," [Speech, November 8, 2003, University of Wisconsin], www.publicairwaves.ca/ [September 27, 2005].

Mulligan, Thomas S., "Nasdaq Joins in Ban of Al Jazeera Stock Market Cites the TV Network's Airing of Images of Dead and Captured U.S. Soldiers," *Los Angeles Times*, March 26, 2003.

Murphy, Jarrett, "Spin War II," *Village Voice*, January 25, 2005.

New York Times v. *United States*, 403 U.S. 713, www.law.umkc.edu [December 13, 2004].

Nichols, Bill and John Diamond, "Speculation, Fact Hard to Separate in Story of Iraq's 'Nuclear' Tubes," *USA Today*, July 31, 2003.

Noah, Timothy, "Fox News Admits Bias!" *Slate Magazine*, May 31, 2005, www.slate.msn.com [October 26, 2005].

Norr, Henry and Goodman, Amy, "*San Francisco Chronicle* Fires Reporter for Attending Peace Protest," *Democracy Now!*, April 24, 2003, www.democracynow.org, August 11, 2003.

Norton-Taylor, Richard, "45 Minutes from a Major Scandal," *Guardian*, February 18, 2004.

Okrent, Daniel, "The Times and Judith Miller's WMD Coverage," *New York Times*, March 25, 2004.

Okrent, Daniel, "Weapons of Mass Destruction? Or Mass Distraction?" *New York Times*, May 30, 2004.

Okrent, Daniel, "An Electrician From the Ukrainian Town of Lutsk," *New York Times*, June 13, 2004.

Okrent, Daniel, "Talking on the Air and Out of Turn: The Trouble with TV," *New York Times*, February 6, 2005.

Okrent, Daniel, "The Public Editor: Briefers and Leakers and the Newspapers Who Enable Them," *New York Times*, November 8, 2005.

Page, Clarence, "A Gulf between Military and Media," *Chicago Tribune*, January 20, 1991.

Panzenbeck, Bob, "Cronkite Can't Rationalize Liberal Media Bias," *College Standard Magazine* (SUNY-Albany), September 8, 2003.

Part Five: Jack Kelley's sources and quotes, USA Today.com, www.usatoday.com [April 24, 2004].

Paterson, Chris, "They Shoot Journalists, Don't They? *Alternet*, August 16, 2005, www.alternet.org August 16, 2005].

Peterson, David, "Abu Ghraib, CBS TV, And American Power," *Z magazine*, May 4, 2004, www.blog.zmag.org [December 16, 2004].

Peterson, David, "Self-Censorship and Torture: Abu Ghraib, CBS and American Power," *Counter Punch*, May 4, 2004, www.counterpunch.org [August 29, 2005].

Pitts, Ryan, "Readers Describe Use of Anonymous Sources as 'double-edge sword,'" *Spokane Spokesman-Review*, June 17, 2005.

Platt, Pam, "On Iraq, Many Misinformed, Uninformed," *Courier-Sentinel*, October 26, 2003.

Podhoretz, John, "A Hitler Mini-series Meant to Bash Bush," *New York Post*, April 9, 2003.

Pollack, Kenneth M., "Spies, Lies, and Weapons: What Went Wrong," Atlantic Online, www.theatlantic.com [March 30, 2004].

Priest, Dana, "Rumsfeld: Criticism at Home, Abroad Encouraging Terrorists," *The Washington Post*, September 8, 2003.

Priest, Dana, "A Clash on Classified Documents," *Washington Post*, March 31, 2004.

Purdum, Todd S. and Patrick E. Tyler, "Top Republicans Break With Bush on Iraq Strategy," *New York Times*, August 16, 2002.

Quincy, Neil Marini, "Says Media Bias is on Display in War Coverage," *Patriot Ledger*, August 7, 2003.

Raimondo, Justin, "Depravity as 'Liberation,'" AntiWar.Com, April 30, 2004.

Rampton, Sheldon and John Stauber, *Weapons of Mass Destruction*, Constable and Robinson Ltd., London, 2003.

Reeves, Richard, "The Decline and Fall of the White House Press Corps," uexpress.com, www.uexpress.com [July 31, 2005].

Reid, Robert H., "American Beheaded on Video, Killers Cite Abuse of Iraqi Prisoners," *Baton Rouge Advocate*, May 12, 2004.

Rhem, Kathleen T., "Military Commander Details Mission That Killed Hussein's Sons," American Information Service, www.defenselink.mil [August 29, 2005].

Ricchiardi, Sherry, "Missed Signals," *American Journalism Review*, August/September 2004, www.ajr.org [August 29, 2005].

Rice, Condoleezza, "Why We Know Iraq is Lying," *New York Times*, January 23, 2003.

Risen, James and David Johnston, "Split at CIA and FBI on Iraqi Ties to Al-Qaeda," *New York Times*, February 2, 2003.

Robbins, Tim, "A Chill Wind is Blowing in this Nation," [Speech given at the National Press Club Washington D.C.], April 15, 2003, www.common-dreams.org, August 14, 2003.

Robertson, Lori, "In Control," *The American Journalism Review*, February/March 2005, www.ajr.org [July 31, 2005].

Rogers, Dick, "Need to Know Put Photos on Page One," SFGate.com, www.sfgate.com [August 29, 2005].

Rosen, Jay, "Stop Us Before We're Briefed Again," *Pressthink*, May 3, 2005, www.journalism.nyu.edu [November 8, 2005].

Roushdy, Ahmad Naguib, "Why Abu Ghraib Matters," *Al-Ahram Weekly*, www.weekly.ahram.irg.eg [December 16, 2004].

Rumsfeld, Donald H., Live Interview With Infinity CBS Radio, November 14, 2002.

Russell, Alec, "As Iraq War Grinds on, US Lapel Pin Loses Appeal," *Daily Telegraph* (London), July 5, 2005.

Sableman, Mark, "The Hidden Camera Conundrum: A Media Lawyer's Perspective," www.rtndf.org [January 20, 2005].

Schecter, Danny, "Why Media Stood Silent When Torture Cases First Came to Light," Common Dreams News Center, May 12, 2004, www.commondreams.org [August 29, 2005].

Schlesinger Jr., Arthur M., "Embracing the True Nature of Patriotism," *Seattle Times*, May 29, 2003.

Schmitt, Eric, "Rumsfeld Says U.S. Has 'Bulletproof' Evidence of Iraq's Links to Al Qaeda," The *New York Times*, September 28, 2002.

Schmitt, Eric and David E. Sanger, "Bush Has Received Pentagon Options on Attacking Iraq," The *New York Times*, September 20, 2002.

Schwartz, John and Fabrikant, Geraldine, "War Puts Radio Giant on the Defensive," *The New York Times*, and March 31, 2003.

Seelye, Katherine Q., "Times Reporter Agrees to Leave the Paper," *New York Times*, November 10, 2005.

Shafer, Jack, "Dealing with Defective Defectors," *Slate Magazine*, April 13, 2004, www.slate.msn.com [January 7, 2004].

Shafer, Jack, "Judy's Turn to Cry," *Slate Magazine*, May 25, 2004, www.slate.msn.com [May 27, 2004].

Shafer, Jack, "The Propaganda President," *Slate Magazine*, February 3, 2005, www.slate.msn.com [July 31, 2005].

Shafer, Jack, "The Jayson Blair Project," *Slate Magazine*, www.slate.msn.com [August 4, 2005].

Shafer, Jack, "The Exorcism of The *New York Times*," *Slate Magazine*, www.slate.com [November 3, 2005].

Shafer, Jack, "The Times Scoops That Melted," *Slate Magazine*, www.slate.com [November 3, 2005].

Shafer, Jack, "Washington Confidential," *Slate Magazine*, March 8, 2004, www.slate.msn.com [November 8, 2005].

Shanker, Thom and David E. Sanger, "U.S. Envisions Blueprint on Iraq Including Big Invasion Next Year," *New York Times*, April 28, 2002.

Shanker, Thomas and Eric Schmitt, "Pentagon Weighs Use of Deception in a Broad Area," *New York Times*, December 13, 2004.

Sidener, Jonathan, "Hackers, Web Hosting Companies become Censors of War Coverage," *San Diego Union-Tribune*, March 28, 2003.

Snowcroft, Brent, "Don't Attack Saddam," *Wall Street Journal*, August 15, 2002.

Snyder, Katherine, "Freedom of Information," *Charleston Gazette*, October 31, 2004.

Solomon, Alisa, "The Big Chill," *Nation*, June 2, 2003.

Solomon, Norman, "The Pentagon Papers," *Z magazine*, July/August 2001, www.thirdworldtraveller.com [December 13, 2004].

Steele, Bob, "Editors & Reporters: What They Owe Each Other," Poynter Online, Posted May 30, 2003, www.poynter.org [November 8, 2005].

Steinbrink, John E. and Jeremy W. Cook, "Media Literacy Skills and the 'War on Terrorism,' " *Clearing House*,Vol. 76, No. 6, July 1, 2003.

Suskind, Ron, "Without a Doubt," *New York Times*, October 17, 2004.

Taha, Kamal, "Iraq Says 'Desperate' US claims of bin Laden Link a Pretext for War," Agence France-Presse, February 12, 2003.

Tait, Richard, "Danish Blue—The War in Iraq Has Polarised the Media in the Most Surprising Quarters," *Financial Times* (London), May 18, 2004.

Turkel, Tux, "Seattle Times Publisher Blasts Media Ownership Concentration as Anti-democratic," *Portland Press Herald*, December 2, 2004.

Ungaro, Joseph M., "Ombudsman: Iraq Coverage not Tripped up by the Wires, *Stars and Stripes*, July 27, 2004, www.estripes.com [July 27, 2004].

Vann, Bill and David North, "Panic and Hysteria Reign at the *New York Times*," World Socialist WebSite, www.wsws.org [August 5, 2005].

The Wall Street Journal, July 12, 2004.

Waldie, Paul, "NYSE shows Al-Jazeera the Door," *Globe and Mail* (South Africa), March 25, 2003.

Watson, Roland and Elaine Monaghan, "US Says Aluminium Tubes Are Evidence of Iraq's Nuclear Goal," *The Times* (London), January 31, 2003.

Weisman, Jonathan, Email, 3/16/2003 4:05:36 PM, Poynter online, www.poynter.org [January 24, 2006].

Weissenstein, Michael, "Publisher: NYT Slow in Correcting Coverage," *Guardian*, October 28, 2005.

Westphal, David, "Conflict with Iraq: Despite questions, American Public Strongly Supports the War," *Naples Daily News*, March 28, 2003, www.naplesnews.com [August 14, 2005].

Wiltrout, Kate, "Stahl of '60 Minutes' Says She Regrets Iraq WMD Stories," *Virginian Pilot*, April 22, 2004.

www.antiwar.com [August 29, 2005].

Wycliff, Don, "Bush Can't Make Case if Networks Aren't Interested," *Chicago Tribune*, January 13, 2005.

Young, Marilyn, "How the Bush Adminsitration Used 9/11 to Advance Its Agenda," *History News Network*, www.hnn.us [January 24, 2006].

Younge, Gary, "Now Dissent Is 'Immoral,' " *Guardian*, June 2, 2003.

Younge, Gary and Julian Borger, "CBS Delayed Report on Iraqi Prison Abuse after Military Chief's Plea," *Guardian*, May 4, 2005.

Zewe, Charles, " 'Infoganda' in Uniform," www.nieman.harvard.edu [January 25, 2006].

INDEX

About the Author

DAVID DADGE is Editor of the International Press Institute in Vienna and author of *Casualty of War: The Bush Administration's Assault on a Free Press* (2004).